Jesuit Studies

JESUIT STUDIES

Work and Education

The Role of Technical Culture
in Some Distinctive Theories of Humanism

John W. Donohue, s.j.

LOYOLA UNIVERSITY PRESS

Chicago, 1959

171.7
D674w

CHRISTO REGI

QUONDAM

FABRO

Education in the United States, as everyone knows, is a vast and complex enterprise. It involves, for instance, two distinct yet complementary school systems, the public and the nonpublic. Each of these runs from the nursery class to the graduate seminar and together they account for a constantly expanding student body which is greater today than the total population of the country was within the memory of men still living. Considering these facts as well as the universal American esteem for education, one is not surprised to find that the relatively new and flexible discipline of the philosophy of education flourishes among us. Indeed, though this discipline has historical antecedents it is to a considerable extent a twentieth-century and even an American development. It tries to relate a generalized discussion of the aims, curriculum, methods, and agencies of formal schooling to a complete philosophy of life and value and so it echoes that older enthusiasm for synoptic world views which has elsewhere gone out of fashion but for which educational practice always has a need. For though the abstract definitions of education may be unenlightening, it is easy enough to see what the reality is. It is, as two such otherwise disparate thinkers as John Dewey and Christopher Dawson agree, the process whereby the older people in a society pass on their total way of life to their children. But when this process absorbs years of the students' lives and employs millions of persons and astronomical sums it becomes more important than ever to evaluate reflectively the culture that is being transmitted and to determine as reasonably as possible the goals and the content of the school experience.

The materials of this book, which in a more technical and extended form were originally the substance of a dissertation presented for the degree of doctor of philosophy in Yale University, constitute a monograph in this general area of the philosophy of education. Occupational psychology assures us that the work we do is most significant both as an index to and as a shaper of our personality. The historian adds that the advance of technology and work's gain in prestige and efficiency during the past millennia are important for civilization and consequently for education. A rounded theory of work can hardly, then, be a matter of indifference to the educator who is concerned with the fulfillment of both the individual and his communities. But a coherent philosophy of this sort itself presupposes the wider perspectives of the philosophies of human nature, of knowledge and of society so that the concept of work's role in education must be logically articulated with an integral interpretation of life. The purpose of these pages is to suggest as much through reflection on certain characteristic approaches to these questions. The writer would like here to thank particularly John S. Brubacher, Halleck professor of history and philosophy of education at Yale University, the Reverend Matthew J. Fitzsimons, S.J., and the Reverend Lorenzo K. Reed, S.J., for the encouragement they provided while the study was under way.

J. W. D.

THE SCHOOL OF EDUCATION,
    FORDHAM UNIVERSITY
May 1, 1959
Feast of St. Joseph the Worker

CONTENTS

xi

PART I

Three Theories
of Work in Education

CHAPTER I

Profile
of the Problem

Isocrates spoke for the professional rhetoricians when he insisted that men transcend the lives of wild beasts precisely because of their power of speech. But within the archaeological perspective, the earliest men are distinguished from brutes by the invention of tools as well as by words. Nevertheless, although philosophers have been impressed by language, they have not been equally appreciative of technology, or industrial science, as a fundamental index of humanity. Perhaps this is because they themselves deal heavily in verbal symbols. At any rate, while a few of them exalted labor, most were only resigned to it as to an unpalatable necessity. Religious insight, on the other hand, has been more enlightened, and Christianity teaches that work is neither a penalty nor a curse, but a fruitful human expression toward which man was naturally oriented even in the days of his innocence. And at all events, work consumes a major portion of most adult lives. Its logical definition may be troublesome to construct, but we can easily point to the thing itself. The economic rewards of labor are by no means the only ones; but men do work in the first place in order that they may live and they are well acquainted with the reality of labor if not with theories interpreting this expenditure of spiritual and bodily energies for the support and enhancement of life.

4 Work and Education

So central an aspect of human experience, therefore, surely ought to be organically related to education. As a matter of fact, it is. Occupations are themselves educators, sometimes for good, sometimes not. Moreover, a great deal of formal schooling is actually vocational, even though this purpose may be veiled and curiously unacknowledged as it assumes forms both more general and more subtle than a program of direct job training. Many Americans go on to high school or college precisely in order to be eligible for better employment, and their expectations have usually not been disappointed. Some day an oversupply of college graduates may scramble this pattern, but in 1954 the secretary of labor could still tell young people that, the more years of schooling they had, the higher their income was likely to be. Vocational preparation, however, whether narrow or broad, is by no means the only possible link between the areas of work and education. If work activities have a distinctive intellectual and moral value, they can be reproduced in the schools for the sake of these benefits quite independently of the economic function. And if labor is indeed one of the chief components of life, it is at least possible that schools might equip youth with a philosophical, and even with a theological, appreciation of its worth, its limitations, and its rank in the total hierarchy of human concerns.

It is not only possible—nowadays it is even rather necessary; for the whole question of work has become more complex and urgent than ever. This is not unexpected, considering the history of western technology, which is a history not only of technocratic expansion but also of a crescendo in the prestige of labor itself, so that by now we are far out on the trajectory of a movement which has wonderfully quickened its speed since the sixteenth century. To say this is not to deny that men of earlier epochs worked with outstanding effectiveness. Some of their achievements, though comparatively rudimentary, were milestones along the road of evolving civilization. We do not know the names of those who first fashioned wheels, domesticated sheep and cattle, or smelted and alloyed metals; but their technical accomplishments were at least relatively impressive. Moreover, the ruins of the Parthenon and Angkor, the furniture of Rome, the screens of feudal Japan and Pueblo pottery, all manifest a beauty and technical brilliance which would be commanding in any age. In the Victoria and Albert Museum there is a superb bowl which an ancient Etruscan artist once fashioned by soldering grains of gold to a surface. No finer work, it has been said, is known from any part of the world at any time.[1]

Nor can it be claimed that an appreciation of the dignity and spiritual values of work is entirely a post-Renaissance phenomenon. There is no doubt that Greek writers usually took a dim view of manual labor, especially if they were city people like Plato and Aristotle—a country gentleman like Xenophon will have some praise for agriculture, at least. Considering the brutal conditions of much industrial toil in classical society, it was easy enough for a philosopher or poet to conclude that work and culture are antagonistic and that labor, howsoever necessary it may be, is a drag on the ideal human life. But there is also reason to suspect that, despite these prejudices, working people themselves, even then, maintained a vigorous pride in their métier and a relish of its values.

An English scholar, for instance, has sifted a mass of non-literary evidence—inscriptions, epitaphs, business records—which shows that in the Greek world from the third century B.C. down to Imperial times there flourished a rich variety of "workingmen's clubs." These were free associations of people with the same occupational interests who originally came together for worship, and later chiefly for social purposes, although the no-

---

[1] Herbert Maryon and H. J. Plenderleith, "Fine Metal-Work," in Charles Singer, E. J. Holmyard, and A. R. Hall, editors, *A History of Technology*, Vol. 1, p. 658. Oxford: Clarendon Press, 1954.

table link between religion and work was never dissolved. The diversity of these groups is surprising: the sacred association of woolworkers at Philadelphia; the most sacred association of fishermen at Cyzicus and of dock porters at Panormus; guilds of weavers, dyers, fullers; linen-workers, goldsmiths and silversmiths, knife makers and bedstead manufacturers. There were clubs for stonemasons, carpenters, farmers, beekeepers, grocers, oil vendors, bakers, millers, and carvers of coral. These guilds were not the counterpart of modern trade unions, for they were not designed to bargain with owners. Their membership, often small and local, included employers and independent craftsmen as well as employees, women as well as men, and slaves alongside citizens. The cohesion of the members was nourished by a pride in their common calling—some, like the tanners and cobblers, made a point of assigning themselves the title of artists— and by the sense of fellowship created among those who followed the same avocation.[2]

When all these necessary qualifications have been made, however, it can still be said that in western society today both the productive power and the ascendancy of work are historically unparalleled. Contemporary man is not disposed to contemn the material universe and its resources when he sees all about him the overwhelming evidence of technological genius in transportation, communication, housing, mass production, and armaments. Our civilization itself, the sociologists tell us, is one of work, and it is held together by the cooperative interaction of people employed in myriad occupations. It has been remarked

---

[2] Marcus N. Tod, *Sidelights on Greek History: Three Lectures on the Light Thrown by Greek Inscriptions on the Life and Thought of the Ancient World*, pp. 30, 71 ff. (Oxford: Basil Blackwell, 1932). The pioneer study of Adriano Tilgher, *Work: What It Has Meant to Men through the Ages*, translated by Dorothy Canfield Fisher (London: George G. Harrap and Company, 1931), although its central theme is sound enough, suffers from generalizations rather too carefree. Tod's researches, for instance, suggest the corrections needed in Tilgher's picture of labor in the Greek world.

that we live, in fact, in an environment more technical than natural—in a world which work has made. We travel by motor, not by horse, and draw water from a faucet, not a stream.[3] This is a relative matter, of course. The poetic transcriptions of air flight in the pages of Saint-Exupéry or Anne Lindbergh suggest that the machine itself can bring men closer to certain natural elements: wind, space, and stars. Still, most of us, most of the time, are at one remove from that world of nature which work has transformed. In such an atmosphere technical culture cannot help but compel attention and admiration. It is not surprising, therefore, that work is much esteemed among us and is judged, not servile, but deeply worthwhile and virtuous. Among average people this conviction may not be clearly articulated, but it is strong and operative. The playboy is universally reprobated. Aristotle might exclude mechanics from citizenship in his model state, but an American president would observe on Labor Day: "America is fortunate in its labor force—which I like to believe is all of us."[4] Indeed, no one works longer, or more intensely, than the wealthy satraps who manage the industrial domains. The border between recreation and work becomes less clearly defined as Americans plunge zealously into the "do-it-yourself" movement. Industry, it seems, has renewed adult interest in craftsmanship by providing reasonably priced power tools and quantities of inexpensive processed material.

This situation, itself, suggests that western man no longer counterpoints labor and leisure, work and contemplation, as de-

---

[3] See Georges Friedmann, *Pour l'unité de l'enseignement: Humanisme du travail et humanités*, p. 6 (Paris: Librairie Armand Colin, 1950) and Theodore Caplow, *The Sociology of Work*, p. 4 (Minneapolis: The University of Minnesota Press, 1954). The comment on the way in which air flight deepens men's consciousness of aspects of nature is owed to a remark by Dr. Robert C. Pollock, professor of philosophy, Fordham University. It appears to be less true of travel by jet planes.

[4] See the text of President Dwight D. Eisenhower's remarks at a Labor Day ceremony at the White House, *New York Times*, September 2, 1956.

cisively as Plato did. The philosopher kings of the *Republic* certainly made no career of indolence. After strenuous preparations they were to spend fifteen years of their ripest maturity in the public service, which would prove them masters of effective action as well as of wisdom. Nevertheless the industrial classes of this mythical state were left out of the election to public education, presumably because their sort of action was too adamant an element to be assimilated and blended into the constitution of the ideal. Even today there are Christian thinkers who reformulate and defend a similar position. It is more usually acknowledged, however, that work can have a religious significance and is not simply the negative pole opposite contemplation. Technology has received no salute more stirring than that from Pius XII in his Christmas Eve discourse of 1953: " 'Inhabit the earth and subject it' (*Gen.* 1, 28) said God to man as He handed creation over to him in temporary heritage. What a long and hard road from then to the present day, when men can at last say that they have in some measure fulfilled the divine command. . . . Now it is clear that all search for and discovery of the forces of nature, which technology effectuates, is at once a search for and discovery of the greatness, of the wisdom, and of the harmony of God."[5]

Yet the question of technical culture is not quite so clear-cut as the considerations thus far might suggest. Certain shadows overcast our actual experience of work and arouse a progressive uneasiness. It is, for instance, precisely the instrumental character of human labor which is a source of trouble. For while technology often has inherent satisfactions of its own, still it is always a tool for the realization of benefits beyond itself. Work, therefore, is rather ambivalent; for although it is a means, it is

---

[5] Pius XII, "Christmas Eve Address: 1953," quoted here from the translation in *Catholic Mind* 52:175-76, March 1954. The original text is in *Acta Apostolicae Sedis* 46:5-16, January 16, 1954.

not necessarily purely utilitarian. If it has intrinsic values, these must be respected, yet kept properly subordinated—and subordinated, indeed, to the proper sort of good. The required balance can be easily upset by two extreme attitudes, each of which, though for different reasons, rejects the ideal of some harmonious rhythm of creative work and fruitful leisure.

There is, for example, the tendency to devaluate work until it is left with only a marketing function. Human toil is esteemed for what it buys, not for what it is. This might be called the Hellenic prejudice revived, but perhaps it would be truer to regard it as a perennial temptation which still beckons despite the triumphs of technology, or even because of them. It is reflected in those advertisements for insurance and annuity plans, baited with the lure of early retirement and buttressed by the assumption that work is, at best, a tedious affair to be done with as soon as possible. Concrete evidence of this spirit rather dashes the zeal of the theoretician who supposes that factory workers are always miserable if confined to routine, piecemeal tasks without significance. A university expert, with wide experience as an industrial consultant, was once watching a woman at work in an electrical-equipment plant. With one hand she plucked light bulbs from a moving belt and with the other swathed them in tissue and thrust them into a carton. It was a matter of three automatic, simple motions. After some conversation the visitor learned that she had been at this post for seventeen years and had no desire to be switched to something "more interesting." "This," she said decisively, "is the best job in the place."

Nevertheless one might guess that, if people do like assembly lines, it is largely for extrinsic and negative reasons. The mechanical operations leave them free to dream or chat. But this only proves that man is more than a worker—is also, in fact, a garrulous and convivial fellow fond of spinning out reveries and hashing over the times with his cronies. There is no real defense here for that industrial depersonalization of labor which robs man of the specific satisfactions of creative craftsmanship and, to that extent, limits his total humanization. It may be added, parenthetically, that production itself is cut when this depersonalization is acute. The practitioners of "human relations in industry" have discovered that efficiency is heightened if there is insight into the importance of the occupation; and they aim, as a popular account put it, to make life more fun by making work more meaningful. Where education is concerned, this negative tendency to see in work only an exchange value fosters unfortunate attitudes, for it is a rather myopic outlook which inclines people to think of technical culture, vis-à-vis the school program, only in terms of a narrow job training.

At the other end of the spectrum are those who, in theory or practice, idolize technology and live for it alone. Sometimes a work mystique of this sort is no more than a makeshift philosophy providing a rough kind of framework in which life can at least be carried on when no other certainties are at hand. A newspaper correspondent, visiting West Germany in 1955, reported that the astounding industrial explosion there was felt, by Germans themselves, to be partly the expression of a "work fanaticism," or "the post-war German opiate"—a way of forgetting the past and ignoring the future.[6] The Freudian analysis uncovers a similar function of work in the lives of those individuals who immerse themselves in their careers to avoid confrontation of personal problems.

More formidable are the reasoned attempts to promote a cultural totalitarianism consciously focused on technology. In Russia and China, so far as one can tell, this is at least the official ideal. At the level of theory this urge to exalt disproportionately the intrinsic values of work finds powerful ideological support in the Marxist and instrumentalist naturalisms. Marx-

---

[6] Albion Ross, "Germany—Report on a Perplexing People." *New York Times Magazine,* p. 69, April 3, 1955.

ism would argue that ultimately, if indirectly, the Gothic cathedral and the American Constitution were expressions of a particular sort of economically determined world view. Scientific naturalism, insisting on the continuity of human and infra-human phenomena, opposes such dualisms as those of man and nature, matter and spirit, art and industry, labor and leisure, philosophical demonstration and empirical experimentation. Distinctions of this kind are invalid, it is said, and must be replaced by the vision of an experience continuum in which ethical inquiry and the painting of a picture are fundamentally no different from the building of a bridge or the search for a new serum; and each of these human expressions is biologically on all fours with the adjustments an animal makes when it hunts for food or flees an enemy. In this view the method of work is thought of as a basic form of the unique method of valid inquiry, the method of hypothesis and test. Both these naturalisms have a pronounced tendency to reduce all culture to technical and scientific culture. Neither Marx nor Dewey would admit as much, but philosophers are frequently unwilling to follow the full flight of their ideas. In educational theory this emphasis is often linked with hostility toward certain traditional humanities—literature, philosophy of a nonpragmatic sort, theology—although the deepest roots of such hostility are in the soil of the naturalistic metaphysics.

When the hardheaded man of affairs shares this exaggerated esteem for work, his educational recommendations are apt to be equally indifferent to the so-called "liberal arts," but for reasons more crass. He will warm to nothing in the school program that is not haloed with an obvious cash value, and his characteristic notion of the relationship between work and education is that of strict vocationalism. In much the same fashion a genuine synthesis of life and work is compromised by the concept of leisure in schemes for maintaining economic equilibrium by constantly stepping up production so that capital may continue to flow and employment stay close to peak. This requires that free time be spent in hasty consumption of the goods produced, lest markets decline. Theories of this sort vitiate the service character of work and misapprehend the nature of man.[7]

A second and immemorial source of equivocation, clouding man's historic experience of labor, is the pain which so often companions it. A great deal of work is hard, or boring, or both; and these aspects can quite obscure the positive valence. A simple love of ease and a relish for the prestige of less arduous arts and professions have not yet been purged, even in Soviet Russia, which is officially an ideocracy grounded on the glorification of labor. In March 1954 the Komsomol, or Young Communist League, held a National Congress in Moscow and A. N. Shelepin, the national secretary of the organization, had some sharp rebukes to deliver under the eye of Premier Malenkov. According to reports Shelepin called for "merciless and decisive war" on the ranks of loafers and hooligans, spongers and parasites, among Soviet youth. They are to be seen, he complained, idling along the city streets dressed like parrots, sporting Tarzan haircuts, neither working nor studying but carousing all the night long. Then, turning from these "aristocrats," the secretary berated in turn those young people who insisted on careers in science or engineering and were unwilling, he said, to dirty their white hands in the hard, skilled labor of the farms.[8] That

---

[7] See Benjamin L. Masse, "Dilemma of More Leisure—or Things," *America* 92:644, March 19, 1955.

[8] *New York Times*, March 21, 1954. A dispatch in the *Times*, September 22, 1954 reported that the Soviet Union was increasing the number of technical training schools opened to graduates of the ten-year urban public school. The course in these schools lasts for one or two years, depending on the intricacies of the trade for which it prepares. In the one-year program classroom lectures and practical work are alternated for six months with only practical work thereafter. The Soviet rulers are trying to divert more young people from universities into these technical institutes, for it is said that in some areas there are more engineers than technicians.

these attitudes were not the prerogative of youth was suggested by dispatches which, that same spring, told of Soviet efforts to pare down the ranks of bureaucrats and get more workers into the factories and fields. The official response to this situation was decisively voiced in a long memorandum on education issued by Premier Nikita S. Khrushchev, September 21, 1958. The chief trouble with the secondary schools, he wrote, lies in the fact of their being divorced from life. They are conducted as though all their students were to be prepared for intellectual pursuits, and consequently both young people and their families show a "lordly, supercilious, incorrect attitude to physical labor." The system must be so reorganized as to send the majority of children to factory or farm work after seven or eight years of schooling. Their education may continue in evening classes, but without forgetting the ideal and practice of useful labor. The preparation of all children for useful work and for the building of communist society must become a sacred slogan.[9]

The Russian difficulties here are comfortably universal; for the satisfactions of labor, unlike those of art or reflection, are frequently blended with the consciously burdensome exertion which the notion of toil implies. The elimination of much of that gross physical pressure is surely a major blessing of machine technology, as even the most determined admirer of homespun and agrarianism must admit. Unfortunately this coin, too, has another side. Mechanized industrial work is itself darkened by serious ambiguities which constitute a third problem complex for any discussion of work in our world. It has often been said that technical progress actually made it possible for the entrepreneur to dump heavier loads on men's backs than ever before. Marx and Engels provided classic descriptions of the witch's

---

[9] The text of the memorandum was issued from Moscow by the Soviet Home Service, September 21, 1958. For a news story on it see *New York Times*, September 22, 1958. Extracts are also available in a translation by Ivan D. London in *School and Society* 86:72-74, February 14, 1959.

broth steaming in the caverns of the nineteenth-century factory. It is true that more recent factual studies in economic history have argued that, despite abuses, the condition of the working class steadily improved throughout that same nineteenth century. Marx himself pointed out that his evidence came from the honest witness borne by English factory inspectors, medical reporters, and commissions of inquiry; and it was actually the public conscience in Britain and America, aroused by testimonies of this sort, which began to sweep out the horrors.

But even after the work week has been reduced to forty hours or so and manufactories have been equipped with the best safety devices and sanitary provisions, and have been set in leafy parks; even when wages are fair, and bulwarked by job and health insurance; even after pensions, skillful collective bargaining, and comanagement schemes, some obstinate problems remain. It would appear that highly mechanized work runs the risk of subjecting the personality to serious frustrations which no amount of familiarity with machines is likely to diminish. For an advanced degree of technological civilization does not seem possible without that division of labor which Marx called detail work and which we know as the assembly line. It is denounced unreservedly in *Capital*, though not so much in itself as in its "bourgeois" form. "It converts the labourer into a crippled monstrosity, by forcing his detail dexterity at the expense of a world of productive capabilities and instincts; just as in the States of La Plata they butcher a whole beast for the sake of his hide or his tallow."[10]

---

[10] Karl Marx, *Capital: A Critique of Political Economy*, translated by Samuel Moore and Edward Aveling, Vol. 1, pp. 396-97 (Chicago: Charles H. Kerr and Company, 1912). Marx quotes here an earlier writer, Ferguson, who said: "Manufactures, accordingly, prosper most where the mind is least consulted, and where the workshop may . . . be considered as an engine, the parts of which are men." And Marx adds that a few eighteenth-century manufacturers preferred, "for certain operations that were trade secrets, to employ half-idiotic persons" *(ibid.)*.

It cannot be said that Marx ever explains convincingly how the communist state of the future is going to retain the technological fruit while ridding itself of this bitter rind. It is easy enough, without undue romanticizing, to see the humanistic values of the independent craftsman's work. He himself made a complete shoe, a table, or a clock. He sketched the plan, picked the tools, and solved the difficulties along the way. But it will hardly help, as Marx himself said, mocking Proudhon, to let the pieceworker on a common pin make the whole pin. If manual labor loses much of its humanizing force when the worker ceases to be a true artisan, can our civilization compensate for this loss by stressing the fellowship of the plant and a technical grasp of the processes of the whole shop? If work in agriculture, business offices, and communications is being rapidly mechanized and assimilated to the industrial patterns of the factory, then a mere variety of occupations—something Marx warmly recommended—is not much use. The Utopianism of the Marxists seems still to blind them at this point. Sure that the advent of classless society and collective ownership will wipe away all defects, they do not diagnose the roots of the trouble closely enough to see that they are not purely economic in character.

Marx believed that members of a collective, owning the means of production, would at last confront the intellectual possibilities involved in production itself. In much the same way Dewey hoped that an understanding of the science applied in technology could make mechanized work a rich source of personal mental development. It may be that careful experimental studies would support these theories, at least in part. But for the moment one can be skeptical. Marx and Dewey never worked in factories. Simone Weil was a philosopher who did do so for a year; and in the journal she kept at the time she noted succinctly: "Nothing is *less* instructive than a machine."[11] Her ex-

---

[11] Simone Weil, *La condition ouvrière*, p. 73. Paris: Gallimard, 1951.

perience in the Renault plant convinced her that it is impossible to work on an assembly line without brutalization; and although her case is hardly typical, still her testimony on this point is unexceptional. It is probably true that, in a commune, individual workers would at least not fear the loss of their jobs to machines. Indeed, they would not be free to idle. Where everyone is an owner, everyone is a worker. In practice this might easily mean that everyone is chained to a pinched and toilsome existence; but even supposing that it resulted, not in an animal farm, but in a workers' paradise, there would still be problems of monotony and spiritual or physical debilitation. The Stakhanovist type might be happy enough, for the heart of this robust industrial athlete is enchanted by mounting goals of ever-greater daily production. But those who seek in work some deeper satisfaction and some realization of their selfhood are hardly likely to be appeased by the spectacle of output schedules spiraling upward. Nor are the extrinsic compensations which the American economy often provides—employees' country clubs, swimming pools, bowling tournaments, picnics, and parties—really relevant. They are not the answer to the problem that might arise should mechanically self-directed, automatic machines some day leave to man only the role of a simple custodian.

All these industrial developments, it is true, also have their golden side, since, for one thing, they dilate the leisure phase of life—or at least are capable of doing so. People today often do have both the time and the means for sampling the pleasures of the arts and crafts, as well as for the expansion of their intellectual horizons. Given this situation, one can wonder if the school ought not to provide some introduction to technical culture aimed at restoring what mechanization is deleting. This aspect of education would form part of the program preparing young people for further exploration of a variety of cultural areas during the leisure hours of their adult life. It would not, of course, meet head-on the central problems of that sort of work which is precisely an economic necessity rather than a hobby. But it might provide the means for authentic compensation if formal work offers small satisfaction, and it might even suggest solutions which would be more than anodynes.

When all these strands are drawn together—the character of labor as a perennial human manifestation, its historic ascent in power and prestige, the ambiguities which always trail it and which industrialism seems to exacerbate—we shall not be surprised to find that the problem of work interests not only the economist, the psychologist, and the sociologist, but also the ethician, the metaphysician, and the theologian. Indeed, reflection and discussion about labor in general and about modern technology in particular are worldwide, though carried on with distinctive variations from place to place.

Many of the essays, for example, on the philosophy and theology of work—essays designed to reassert the human dignity of technological enterprise—are by French writers. There are several possible explanations for this. It is probably true that among these people the countryman and the small craftsman have kept alive a tradition of excellence in horticulture and the useful arts and, consequently, an implicit awareness of work's humanistic potential. At the same time, the official cultural tradition, especially in its academic form, has been dominantly intellectualistic in a rather constricted sense. The education of man has meant the cultivation of intelligence through studies in literature, history, "pure" science, and philosophy. But if culture is defined exclusively in these terms, the workman is left to sink with his labor below the level of the fully human. Any ideal of reciprocity between work and contemplation is suffocated if their distinction, real though it is, be interpreted as fundamental incompatibility.

In recent decades, therefore, alert European thinkers in the university world and in the Church have sought to re-establish lines of communication between the zones of work and those of intellectual culture and religion. It has been realized, for instance, that technology can itself create that favorable climate in which other human splendors flower. Thus Giorgio LaPira, the scholar mayor of Florence, told an American journalist: "In the United States there are both greater production and spiritual values. . . . The elementary problems in your country have already been solved. There is a high standard of living which permits religion and contemplation to develop. But in Italy the people are immediately occupied with the task of finding bread."[12] And, of course, those who look for an integral philosophy and theology of work want to do more than underscore this obvious instrumental office. They also hope to set forth convincingly the humanistic values of production itself.

Americans, conventionally caricatured as hopelessly infatuated with industry and its fruits, do not feel the same compulsion to recover a sense of these values, for they have never really lost it. It is more common, in fact, to fear that unbalanced enthusiasm for technological expansion may drag us down to the service of crude aspirations and the neglect of the loftiest idealism. "I wonder," said Adlai Stevenson at Columbia in June 1954, "if we are in danger of falling into a spirit of materialism in which the aim of life is a never-ending increase of material comfort, and the result a moral and religious vacuum."[13] There is also fear that in a machine universe the real experience of work's unique rewards may be seriously diminished. Considerable interest is focused, therefore, on the study of the sociological and psychological effects of progressive mechanization. Much as they appreciate the power of technology, Americans would, perhaps, hesitate to see it developed to a point where the joy of creativity is volatilized. We are told that in the auto-

---

[12] C. L. Sulzberger, "Six Vignettes That Tell Italy's Story." *New York Times Magazine,* pp. 15, 59, May 16, 1954.
[13] Quoted in *New York Times,* June 6, 1954.

matic kitchen of the future the housewife will simply unpackage frozen foods and mixes, and bake or broil a whole dinner in an electronic oven that does the job in seconds. In itself this may be quite desirable, but as a symbol of tomorrow it is not wholly reassuring. Shortly after the First World War, Willa Cather told a lecture audience in Omaha:

> Restlessness such as ours, success such as ours, do not make for beauty. Other things must come first; good cookery, cottages that are homes, not playthings; gardens, repose. These are first-rate things, and out of first-rate stuff art is made. It is possible that machinery has finished us as far as this is concerned. Nobody stays at home any more; nobody makes anything beautiful any more.[14]

This is, to be sure, a distinctively personal view expressed with some rhetorical heightening. Besides, the picture after World War II was rather different. It has been often remarked that the men who returned from military service in the late 1940's had a passion for domesticity. They had been to the ends of the earth, and now they wanted to settle down, raise a family, paint and plaster, and putter about a house and scrap of lawn all their own. Nevertheless the observation of the great artist quoted here is, if not a transcript of our situation, at least a warning which deserves consideration.

It is hard to tell what exactly the Asians think about these questions of work and modern industry. Much of the labor they know, even now, is physically so painful and economically so unrewarding that they would probably regard as fantastic any talk about its possibilities for humanization, to say nothing of sanctification. The Asiatic intellectual, moreover, is never tired of caustically rebuking Americans for their alleged preoccupation with material comfort and of assuring them, top-loftily, that their nylon and lipstick and chewing-gum civilization is no

---

[14] Quoted in E. K. Brown, *Willa Cather: A Critical Biography*, p. 227. New York: Alfred A. Knopf, 1953.

match for ways of life two thousand years old. This indictment is ironic, for all over the Asiatic sphere the masses of people are striving to exchange for these millennial patterns just that sort of comfortable, industrialized world which their spokesmen sometimes affect to scorn. Asians want the more humane world that technology can build, as President Diem of South Vietnam told the United States Congress in May 1957. It is true, of course, that this is not all they want. Even in China the characteristic Marxist cult of labor is joined to an enthusiasm for a "people's" culture and education. Writing in 1927, Mao Tse-tung declared that 90 per cent of the Chinese people "have no culture or education" although it was "the peasants' sweat and blood" which created those refinements which the landlords had pre-empted. It was the virtue of the peasants' revolution, he claimed, to have extended opportunities for schooling and culture to those who had never known them.[15]

So far as other countries can tell, at any rate, the Asians are moving as fast as they can away from that ancient tradition which consigned the bulk of people to a life totally consumed by primitive toil. Perhaps they, too, would relish the synthesis of creative and reflective action, of labor and leisure, which modern technology brings within reach. But in their struggle for this happy amalgam, will they not also encounter those distinctive ambiguities which presently trouble men of the Atlantic nations? It is the paradox of industrial technology that, even as it offers the peoples of depressed areas the chance to become fully human, it also involves them in the risk of new corruptions should the machine slip their control.

This is a formidable welter of questions; and many of them will hardly be touched upon here, much less explored. But if the problem of work in education is to be formulated, even at the

---

[15] Mao Tse-tung, *Selected Works*, Vol. 1, p. 56. New York: International Publishers Company, 1954.

level of theory, it has seemed best to advert to its real and total context. It is wise to begin with an acknowledgment of these plus-and-minus facets of work which make it easy to pitch off into extremes. Work can be boring, and it can be bitter; and consequently those who sing its praises do so uneasily because they cannot forget the gap between the ideal they rhapsodize and the reality many men endure. At the same time, thoughtful people today realize that work is more than a necessary evil. The position and influence of organized labor suggest as much. It would be naive to ascribe this position simply to an ethical appreciation of the dignity of human labor; but surely workingmen have been sustained in their struggle for social justice by an awareness of their pivotal role in our civilization, and they won their campaigns partly because ownership, government, and informed public opinion had reached the same conviction.

Against this complex background, then, the question of basic education for work is posed. Faced with it, several different postures may be struck. Without urging the label, we might call Hellenic that tradition which thinks of education as, above all else, the education of speculative intelligence and aesthetic sensibility. In practice this does not mean that bodily vigor, for instance, is neglected, but simply that it is cultivated for the sake of the soul, just as character education is not forgotten, but provided for, by an equation of knowledge with virtue. The *Republic* prescribed for the military class both music and gymnastics, but the function of each was the formation of the brave spirit. In theory at least, work experience can be accommodated here if it can be shown to contribute significantly to moral and intellectual growth. But this attitude passes over more easily into one of exaggerated intellectualism, in which education is understood in terms of rational and bookish exercise.

The classical Marxist accent is directly opposite. Within this perspective man's essential distinction from the brutes is linked to his labor. Logically, then, education would aim to cultivate this characteristic work power. "Spirit," if the word must be retained at all, is only a nuance of matter that emerges as workers realize the full range of their capacities.

The Christian outlook differs from all of these. It does not think of man as purely corporeal, nor as an imprisoned spirit, nor as the uneasy dualism formed by juxtaposition of body and soul, but rather as a natural composite, flowering from the vital union of two essential principles, one spiritual and one material. Christian education is, therefore, above all the education of *man*, of the total human person; and it seeks the actualization of all his virtualities—those for work as well as those for contemplation. It does not hope to solve the problem of technological enterprise either by exaggerating or by minimizing its role. It hopes, instead, for a harmony which at its deepest level must be effected by religion, since it is only within the religious dimension that the full instrumentality of labor is grasped and its painful aspects rendered intelligible.

It is clear enough, therefore, that to ask about the role of work in the humanistic formation of man is to enter inevitably on a whole set of perennial and crucial disputes. It may lead to inquiry about the aims of education—always the stimulant of interminable debate. It raises questions about the nature of man himself. Is he essentially *nous,* a captive soul? Or is he merely the primate who learned to work and built a thousand cultures as he grew? Supposing that he is neither exclusively the one nor the other, do all his perfections have, nonetheless, a real bond with the life of intelligence? And even if the aim of education is principally a growth in charity and wisdom, can the work career of an ordinary man contribute to this?

Around these themes buzz the practical school issues. Shall the school educate for work, or for leisure, or for both under a single formality? Man is certainly one who works. But not everyone will agree that he is only, or even chiefly, a worker. How, then, educate the complete man who is both worker and more than worker? Is vocational training the only preparation, or even the best preparation, for the work of maturity? What are the vocational values of the liberal arts and the actual intellectual exercise of traditional schooling? Should there be craftsmanship classes, work experience in industry, agriculture, and community projects? If so, when and for how long, and with what sort of administrative framework? Or it may be objected that the common schools are busy enough with languages, sciences, and social studies. Why try to squeeze more material into a program already sadly overloaded? The objection, to be sure, is somewhat off center if it assumes that the school must become the sole educator for work, but it serves a good purpose if it reminds us that other agencies also have their responsibilities.

There are problems of method. Granted that we wish to include in the total humanization of men some education for and through work, we must still inquire as to how this can best be done. There are problems of guidance—in fact, the problem of juvenile delinquency may be partly the problem of vigorous young people bursting with energy and initiative for which no creative outlet exists. In any case, it is always important to help students select some suitable occupation, and it is equally important to prepare them to savor work's joys and appreciate its austerity and discipline. Indeed, what is more vital in this whole affair than the restoration of enthusiasm for work itself if this has been lost? On the other hand, people must be somehow armed to meet the pressures of industrialized labor.

All such riddles have this in common, that they return thought, finally and firmly, to the philosophical problems lying at their heart. In the pages that follow there is no attempt to answer these practical questions, nor even to solve definitively the more radical ones. We attend, instead, to a sort of dialogue on the humanizing function of work. It is a dialogue in which the voices are those of celebrated protagonists of certain key positions in this whole matter, with Christianity serving both as contributor and moderator. The speakers have been selected because they create a pattern which is not wholly arbitrary. Although both Marx and Veblen, for instance, stressed the relationship between economic conditions and ideologies, it is Marx who figures here because his thought has been so obviously influential. Although both Dewey and Bergson reflect on the development of human intelligence through work, it is the former who is of most significance for the American scene. The positions represented range roughly from left to right; from Karl Marx, whose thought represents the high-water mark of the tendency to exalt work for its own sake, to twentieth-century Americans echoing that Greek conviction which puts the value of work in its purchase of leisure for intellectual pursuits. Sometimes these voices harmonize; sometimes they are complementary, sometimes dissident. Communism will incline to see in man only *homo faber;* traditional humanism only *homo sapiens;* while pragmatism will tend to equate *faber* with *sapiens.* The Christian interpretation of life, from which as a base this review is projected, recognizes both aspects and acknowledges their mutual influence, but maintains a real distinction between the two, linked to the real distinction between matter and spirit dynamically constructing the unified human personality.

The thinkers represented here are not so much concerned with showing *how* work may fit into a balanced life and education as with showing *why* it should thus fit, and where its significance lies. This concern with the "metaphysical mysteries" of craftsmanship and technology is, to be sure, often deprecated, particularly by those social scientists for whom theoretical discussion is simply the waste of good time which might better be spent on practical effort. Everyone agrees, it may be said, that we need a spirituality of work, an understanding of work as the means of ethical maturation, and an instrument of personal development. Indeed, these are clichés by now. What we most require are concrete methods for achieving those highly generalized goals. The objection is not without force, yet it may be that some consideration of the *why* will light up the *how*. It is worthwhile, after all, to see whether there really are distinctive values in work which are worth pursuing and how these are to be located in a wider synthesis. This may actually clarify the question of educating for an ordered possession of these real goods. The theories surveyed in the following pages are, in each instance, intimately related to a systematic philosophy, and they will not recommend themselves unreservedly to those who find the total system invalid. But the fact of these relationships makes one point plain. In the history of thought such themes as those of God, life, religion, civilization, freedom, love, and spirit have long been pivotal. But the idea of work is also, in its own way, one of these philosophical neurons whose fibers reach to every part of the speculative structure. This may serve, in turn, to suggest just how central the question of work's involvement in education really is.

CHAPTER II

The Marxian Apotheosis
of Work

In the mass of writings left by Karl Marx there is a great deal about labor but relatively little about education. Nevertheless a quantitative measure would be misleading in this case; for as the implications of Marxism are drawn out, the educational ideal emerges as highly important. Like most communist ideals, this one is a goal of the future, and in *Capital* Marx credited Robert Owen with predicting its structure. Education in the new age would be universal and compulsory and would develop the children in three arenas: in the school through academic instruction, in the gymnasium through calisthenics, and in the factory or on the farm through serious participation in productive work. To put it another way, the labor force, instead of encompassing about half the total population as it did in the United States between wars, would enlist all except the very old, the very young, and the sick. According to Marx this is not only a means of increasing industrial efficiency; it is also the only method of producing fully developed human beings.

The third phase of that program makes it still seem novel enough, for not even the Russians have attempted to carry it through completely. Yet Marx's original recommendations were not nearly so sweeping as they might have been if he had carried his principles to their limit. This is clear if one recalls the absolute centrality of work in the economics, the metaphysics, and the philosophical anthropology of Marxism. When the curtain rises on the Marxian vision of history, men are found already at work. Naturally so. For the basic condition of life, and consequently of any history, is that men must sustain their existence, must procure food and shelter if they are to live at all. It is, in fact, precisely this productive activity which decisively marks them off from the beasts. In 1846, more than a decade before *On the Origin of Species* appeared, Marx and Engels wrote: "Men can be distinguished from animals by consciousness, by religion or anything else you like. They themselves begin to distinguish themselves from animals as soon as they begin to *produce* their means of subsistence, a step which is conditioned by their physical organization."[1] Many years later Engels fleshed out this thesis with Darwinian detail in an ingenious essay on "The Part Played by Labor in the Transition from Ape to Man." There he postulated with considerable imaginative itemization the ascent of a favored anthropoid to a human plateau as its paw developed into a hand. Clambering about among the trees, gathering food, and whistling stones at intruders, this primate first discovered the special capacities of its forefeet and then the use of rudimentary tools. Because these tools made ambitious work projects possible, the gregarious hominids hatched plans requiring mutual communication and so, observed Engels, language itself originated from and in the process of labor.

It is a clever if highly presumptive exercise in the apriorism for which Engels had rather a weakness. (He once wrote to tell Marx that a number of applications of the dialectic to physics and chemistry had come into his head while he was lying in bed

---

[1] Karl Marx and Friedrich Engels, *The German Ideology*, edited by R. Pascal, p. 7 (New York: International Publishers Company, 1947). A few pages later the authors speak of the human need for food and shelter and observe: "The first historical act is thus the production of the means to satisfy these needs, the production of material life itself" (*ibid.*, p. 16).

that morning.) The nuclear Marxian thesis on labor, however, had been determined quite independently of Darwin and its logical corollaries were first sketched in the 1840's. Just as specifically human history begins with human work, so too, Marx believed, beneath the thousand and one shifting manifestations of art, philosophy, politics, law, and religion the underlying ground, and the ultimately decisive element of this history, has always been man's productive activity. Nor is this all. For when he looked to the future, Marx was convinced that he saw a new society rising from the rubble of the crucial conflict between proletariat and *bourgeoisie*. Although it might not be the perfect community, this new order would be, at least, the best that had yet existed. It would be most suitably characterized in terms of its apotheosis of labor:

> In a higher phase of communist society, after the enslaving subordination of individuals under division of labour, and therewith also the antithesis between mental and physical labour, has vanished, after labour has become not merely a means to live but has become itself the primary necessity of life, after the productive forces have also increased with the all-round development of the individual, and all the springs of co-operative wealth flow more abundantly—only then can the narrow horizon of bourgeois right be fully left behind and society inscribe on its banners: from each according to his ability, to each according to his needs.[2]

---

[2] Karl Marx, "Critique of the Gotha Programme," in Karl Marx, *Selected Works*, edited by C. P. Dutt, Vol. 2, p. 566 (New York: International Publishers Company, 1936). An interesting clarification of the economic interpretation of history is given in one of Engels' letters: "According to the materialist conception of history the determining element in history is *ultimately* the production and reproduction in real life. More than this neither Marx nor I have ever asserted. If therefore somebody twists this into the statement that the economic element is the *only* determining one, he transforms it into a meaningless, abstract and absurd phrase. . . . We make our own history, but in the first place under very definite presuppositions and conditions. Among these the economic ones are finally decisive" (Engels to J. Bloch, September 21, 1890, in Karl Marx and Friedrich Engels, *Selected Correspondence, 1846-1895*, translated by Dona Torr, pp. 475-76. New York: International Publishers Company, 1942).

Here in a true sense man's labor is both the source and the goal of his whole story. It is, as Marx and Engels put it in *The German Ideology*, "the language of real life." The philosophical exaltation of work reaches a peak when the problem of its place in a scheme of values is solved by making human labor itself the Master Value. The Greek tradition is overthrown. Man's unique and noblest expression is not now a lofty contemplation transcending matter, but concrete thought about and action upon the encircling material world for the sake of producing human existence by producing the means of subsistence. It is in and through this very action, indeed, that man *becomes* man, just as it is work which creates the human community. Consequently, productive labor ought logically to be at the heart of education's humanistic enterprise.

Still, Marx himself had been formed in the nineteenth-century German tradition of classical humanism, and one cannot help suspecting that his own intellectual history left him with a strong attraction for the speculative and affective approaches to reality even though his formal philosophy was emphatically pragmatic. He insisted, it is true, that the scholar must not be immured in his study like a maggot in a cheese, but he also believed that scientific research should be pursued for its own sake, as Lafargue, his disciple and son-in-law, testified. When he set himself to train up communist leaders for the future, the training itself was violently intellectual. He drove the cold and hungry revolutionaries to the reading room of the British Museum, crying, "Learn! Learn!" Years later one of them recalled how he had been made to study Spanish with Marx presiding over daily translations from *Don Quixote*. Marx himself could write correct French and English as well as his own German. He read omnivorously, and not only in philosophy and economics. Lafargue said he knew Heine and Goethe by heart, that there was a veritable Shakespeare cult in the Marx family, that Marx cherished Dante and Burns, and that for recreation he used to have two or three novels going at once. Nor was this passion for the life of thought and imagination purely utilitarian. Although Marx did urge language studies with the reflection, "A foreign language is a weapon in the struggle for life," Lafargue could also say of him: "Thinking was his supreme enjoyment. I have often heard him quote from Hegel, the master of the philosophy of his youthful days, the saying: 'Even the criminal thought of a scoundrel is grander and more sublime than the wonders of the heavens.' "[3]

It is possible, therefore, that his own classical education turned Marx unconsciously away from the rigorous concept of an exclusively polytechnical formation, although such a concept seemed dictated by his theses. His life had had its own dialectical design: a youth fervently engaged with literature and philosophy; a gradual involvement in what he described as discussions of so-called material interests; and at last, following turbulent expulsions from one European capital after another, permanent residence in London and the settled synthesis of study and action until death. The tone of the household of his boyhood was set by Karl's father, Heinrich, a man who had renounced Judaism for state Lutheranism and who was once described by a granddaughter as a typical eighteenth-century Frenchman knowing his Voltaire and Rousseau by heart. The temper of his comfortable ménage was, as Lenin put it, cultured but not revolutionary and cultured Karl Marx became, although also revolutionary. His academic training in school and university was very thorough, and all his life he kept extending his researches in some favored fields while promptly dismissing others—religion for one.

This sort of intellectual effort made him, indeed, a repository of many of the ideologies of his day. Lenin, in a well-known

---

[3] Paul Lafargue, "Reminiscences of Marx," in Marx, *Selected Works*, Vol. 1, p. 87. These reminiscences were published in the *Neue Zeit* in September 1890.

sketch, claimed that Marx "was the genius who continued and completed the three chief ideological currents of the nineteenth century, represented respectively by the three most advanced countries of humanity: classical German philosophy, classical English political economy, and French socialism combined with French revolutionary doctrines."[4] In any event, Marx was always very much a man of the nineteenth century; both the product and the critic of his age, and critic because product. In his graveside comment on the day of Marx's burial at Highgate, Engels said that the two greatest discoveries of his friend were those of the law of evolution in history and of surplus value. It is conventional but true to add that both of these fit most naturally into the nineteenth-century context, although this is not to deny that the figure of Marx is larger than its frame.

The man himself had a personality which caused his partisans some embarrassment and has fascinated students with a flair for psychographs. Marx's adult years were filled with tribulations: exile, poverty, pain. Certainly he had an ample share of trouble. His letters are full of the gray details: unpaid bills, personal vendettas, hemorrhoids, fatigue. There were great family tragedies in the deaths of an infant daughter in 1852 and of a cherished nine-year-old son who died in his father's arms a few years later. Perhaps the repellant side of Marx's nature— his abuse of opponents, rupture of friendships, indifference to the sufferings of those closest to him, and all that even some who knew him well called heartlessness—is better viewed against this background. He has been dismissed out of hand as a misanthrope, yet he made an unusually happy marriage and many enduring friendships. His closest associates drew an attractive picture of the aging scholar fond of cigars and spicy foods, keeping his mass of papers untidily, and wearing a pathway in

---

[4] V. I. Lenin, "Karl Marx," in Marx, *Selected Works*, Vol. 1, p. 23. This article was published in 1919 in the seventh edition of the *Granat Encyclopaedia*.

the old carpet as he paced in thought. They lingered over the image of an indulgent father sailing paper boats with his daughters and riding his grandson pickaback; the head of the household leading picnics to Hampstead Heath, searching for wild hyacinths in spring and chestnuts in fall, and on the way home singing old patriotic songs: "O Strassburg, O Strassburg, du wunderschöne Stadt." This portrait needs to be set alongside the more conventional one of the ogre, "the best hated man of his time," for in its own way it suggests, contrary to one of Marx's pivotal themes, that there is, after all, much more to any man than "relations of production" can finally explain.

THE GUIDING THREAD

Though Marx was educated in the European tradition, his humanism of work is interesting because it is rather untraditional. It maintains, in effect, that there is really no need to strain for a harmonious synthesis of work and life, for work *is* life. A vigorous enough formula, certainly, and one that deserves closer inspection. First, however, some simple boundaries ought to be staked out.

Only yesterday Soviet communism proposed Marx-Engels-Lenin-Stalin as moments of a perfectly continuous process in which the undoubted evolution is homogeneous and immanent. Stalin, indeed, once told some American visitors that Lenin had neither added any new principles to Marxism nor abolished any of the old but had simply been "a loyal and consistent pupil of Marx and Engels."[5] The clamorous existence, however, of plenty of anti-Soviet Marxists invalidates these bland assumptions. It is better, therefore, to question directly Marx himself and avoid the acidulous controversies that divide his commentators. Lenin,

---

[5] J. Stalin, "From the Interview with the First American Labour Delegation in Russia," in Marx, *Selected Works*, Vol. 1, pp. 74, 79. The interview took place September 9, 1927.

for instance, understood Marxism as the triumph of an ultimate truth. "The teaching of Marx is all-powerful because it is true. It is complete and harmonious, providing men with a consistent view of the universe, which cannot be reconciled with any superstition, any reaction, any defence of bourgeois oppression."[6] The exegesis of American naturalism, on the other hand, finds such a reading intolerable, for it is persuaded that Marx embodied a fundamental pragmatism inimical to any absolutes.

What one looks for, then, is a summary built up from Marx's own words with some recourse to Engels for corroboration or elucidation. This is not to suggest that Engels was notably inferior to Marx or that his views were essentially different. Despite his modest disclaimers, Engels had a vigorous intelligence capable of vast efforts, and it is well known that by reflection on English industrial conditions he had arrived independently at the central intuition of his and Marx's theory: the role of economic life as the ultimate determinant of human history. But a focus on Marx is not unreasonable, for it is he who must always bear among communists the title which the schoolmen gave Aristotle: *Philosophus*. For Marx, said Engels in a familiar tribute, could have done without the others, but not they without him. "Marx stood higher, saw further, and took a wider and quicker view than all the rest of us. . . . Without him the theory would not be what it is today. It therefore rightly bears his name."[7]

But even a focus on Marx has to be sharpened, since there are several Marxes. It is Marx the philosopher who claims our

---

[6] V. I. Lenin, "The Three Sources and Three Component Parts of Marxism," in Marx, *Selected Works*, Vol. 1, p. 54. The three sources are the German philosophy, English political economy, and French socialism. The three component parts are the philosophy of materialism, the theory of surplus value as the cornerstone of economics, and the doctrine of class struggle.

[7] Friedrich Engels, "Ludwig Feuerbach and the Outcome of Classical German Philosophy," in Marx, *Selected Works*, Vol. 1, p. 451, n. 1.

attention, rather than the economist, the political scientist, or the architect of revolution. Of course these formalities, inseparable in the living thinker, are interconnected and can be only imperfectly abstracted. Nevertheless there is good reason to maintain that the philosophical thought was the substratum of all the rest. To be sure, there has been some bootless dispute as to whether Marx was a philosopher at all. He and Engels liked best to style themselves "men of science," and there are irate passages in *The German Ideology* which disparage philosophy. But as Marx himself once observed, "You cannot abolish philosophy without putting it into practice." Besides, *The German Ideology* is itself a philosophical exercise aimed at the target of Hegelian idealism, whether of the "old" or "young" variety. It is opposed both to the orthodox defenders of the self-realizing Absolute and to those who announced, indeed, the "putrescence of the absolute spirit" but were themselves idealists of a different breed. Its wrath is reserved, therefore, for any system which puts the idea first and makes principles or categories generate conclusions—systems, Marx and Engels said, which descend from heaven to earth. By contrast their own method is to travel the other way by starting with an existential datum, real men in a real world. They claimed to formulate *their* philosophical conclusions, many of them general and abstract enough, from precise empirical observation; and with such an intention, at least, many realists would agree.

In epistemology as well as in method the Marxian stance is again realistic in its conviction that we do indeed know an actual world. Hume and Kant were quite wrong, said Engels, and practice proves them so. Nineteenth-century chemists, for instance, concluded from their studies that a dye could be produced more cheaply from coal tar than from madder roots and, sure enough, it was. Their very success proves the "correctness of our conception of a natural process." Marx, too, favored this combination of a psychological realism and a pragmatic criterion. On the one hand, he rejected Hegel's opinion that the real world is simply the external, phenomenal form of the Idea. "With me, on the contrary," he wrote, "the ideal is nothing else than the material world reflected by the human mind, and translated into forms of thought."[8] On the other hand, his pragmatic bent is suggested by the second of the celebrated theses he jotted down on Feuerbach:

> The question whether objective truth can be attributed to human thinking is not a question of theory but is a practical question. In practice man must prove the truth, i.e., the reality and power, the "this-sidedness" of his thinking. The dispute over the reality or non-reality of thinking which is isolated from practice is a purely scholastic question.[9]

From their ruminations these two realistic, empirical, and pragmatic thinkers developed a metaphysics of materialism which is the essential framework of their sort of humanism. It may be true, as Marx declared, that the philosophers have only interpreted the world whereas the point is to change it, but the authentic communist must first do his homework on theory. Every sincere worker, said Lenin, would include among his "household books," along with the *Manifesto*, Engels' two speculative treatises on materialism: *Ludwig Feuerbach* and the *Anti-Dühring*. Lenin himself found it useful to preface a summary of Marx's economic teaching with a "brief outline of his world conception in general" because the two doctrines were so unified and consistent.

This Marxian cosmos can be entered at several points, but educators will be naturally inclined to start with its theory of man and his concrete situation and radiate from there outwards. Such an approach fits the system itself very well. For human

---

[8] Engels' comments are to be found in Marx, *Selected Works*, Vol. 1, pp. 431-33 and Marx's in Marx, *Capital*, Vol. 1, p. 25, a passage forming part of the preface to the second edition.

[9] Karl Marx, "Theses on Feuerbach," in Marx, *Selected Works*, Vol. 1, p. 471.

history, said Marx, means men, and its first questions are about
the physical organization of these entities and about their relation to the rest of nature. It was precisely while meditating on
such matters in Paris and Brussels, 1844-1845, that Marx arrived at the insight which dynamically integrated his previous
thinking and served, he said, as the "guiding thread" of all his
future studies. This was, of course, the celebrated concept of
historical materialism which sees in man's economic life the
crucial factor of human existence and history. But the Marx who
uncovered this thread in 1845 was already possessed of some
highly significant convictions, one inspired by Hegel, the other
by Feuerbach, which were even more basic for his thought.

In the first place, by the time he finished his youthful doctoral dissertation on the "Difference between the Democritic and
Epicurean Philosophies of Nature," Marx had rejected any
form of theism. Democritus' naive mechanism, indeed, with its
lack of some immanent source of progressive movement, was
hardly an acceptable version of materialism, and Marx would
later try to mend it by applying an enormously fecund Hegelian
principle. But although Hegel is the massive genius whose wings
shadow so many pages in both Marx and Dewey, his doctrine
of the Absolute Spirit was, after a time, rejected by both. Such
a rejection meant liquidation of faith in that God so unfortunately identified with Hegel's Absolute. Predictably enough, the
vacuum this denial created came to be filled by a new faith in
man himself as the capstone of reality.

This shucking of religious belief does not seem to have been
any great matter for Marx personally, and certainly the central
theological questions which have so preoccupied many other
philosophers are all but ignored by him. A few derisive remarks, an occasional denunciation, suffices. "Man makes religion," Marx commented once; "religion does not make man."
And as soon as men found their feet in the world, he thought,
they would get rid of this paralyzing projection of their own

fears, this "Spirit of spiritless conditions . . . the opium of the people."[10] Engels, however, was more sensitive to the importance of religion, not merely as a historical factor but precisely as a crucial question posed for the individual. For Engels had been a devout youth and he had not lost the pietistic faith of his boyhood without travail and tears. Consequently in *Ludwig Feuerbach* he makes the Marxist position explicit by raising the question: "Is there a spiritual being with primacy over matter?" Or, more pointedly, "Did God create the world or has it existed eternally and independently?" All who uphold the primacy of spirit are lumped together as idealists and Hegel is made their prophet. Those for whom material nature is primary are distributed among the various materialistic schools. And this, Engels concludes, is all idealism and materialism properly mean, for his rude simplification allows no place for a philosophy both realistic and theistic.

Marx devised a rather distinctive formula for this basic materialism, and on several occasions Engels devoted his gifts for popularization to its exposition. In the *Anti-Dühring*, for instance, he first sweeps his readers back to the dawn of western philosophical history when the Greeks of 500 B.C. faced up to a perennial question. The chief object of human reflection should be life itself, so infinitely rich, varied, complex, and dynamic. Yet how can one study this multiple and processive reality except by plucking scraps from the turbulent stream for a detached and detailed investigation? Such piecemeal analysis is not without value; for as Engels observed in *Ludwig Feuerbach*, one must first know what a thing is before observing the changes it undergoes. Nevertheless it is always a great loss if

---

[10] Karl Marx, "A Criticism of the Hegelian Philosophy of Right," in *Karl Marx, Selected Essays*, translated by H. J. Stenning, pp. 11-12 (New York: International Publishers Company, 1926). On the young Marx of the doctoral dissertation see H. P. Adams, *Karl Marx in His Earlier Writings*, pp. 37-38 (London: George Allen and Unwin, 1940).

the primitive but essentially accurate conception of being as "becoming," which Heraclitus formulated, is forgotten.

What Engels was pleased to label the metaphysical mode of thought consisted, he said, in just such a neglect of process and of the whole web of relations intrinsic to the nature and existence of things. With Bacon and Locke this natural-science method of immobilizing and morseling natural objects and processes, of considering them "not in their life, but in their death," was grafted onto philosophy, and its ashen fruit was a lifeless, useless conceptualism. Into this desert the post-Kantian thought, culminating in Hegel, turned an irrigating stream when it rediscovered the dialectical flux at the core of reality. The whole universe was understood to exist in a condition of ceaseless change, and in this light one can appreciate the functional character of history as "the process of development of humanity itself." It will be the main business of thought to plot the stages of this human process and "to trace out the inner regularities running through all its apparently fortuitous phenomena."[11]

Hegel himself never succeeded in this philosophical map making. His system is genially dismissed as a "colossal miscarriage" because its perverse idealism tried to explain process in terms of the evolution of images of the Idea "existing somewhere or other already before the world existed." But Hegel's emphasis on "becoming" and his theory of its dialectical character manifested in nature and human history was a permanent acquisition for those new materialists who did properly under-

---

[11] Friedrich Engels, *Herr Eugen Dühring's Revolution in Science*, translated by Emile Burns, p. 30 (New York: International Publishers Company, n. d.). For this same emphasis on change see Friedrich Engels, *Dialectics of Nature*, translated by Clemens Dutt, pp. 13-14 (New York: International Publishers Company, 1940): "Thus we have once again returned to the point of view of the great founders of Greek philosophy, the view that the whole of nature, from the smallest element to the greatest, from grains of sand to suns, from protista to men, has its existence in eternal coming into being and passing away, in ceaseless flux, in unresting motion and change."

stand what the ontological stuff really is. As a matter of fact, says Engels, science is proving daily that all nature's processes are dialectical. Just as Hegel freed the conception of history from metaphysics and made it dialectical, so Darwin has swept out the metaphysical conception of nature and has shown that the whole organic realm from vegetables to man moves, not in an endless cycle, but in a rhythm of true historical evolution. Engels had conveniently overlooked the fact that the unpredictable Darwinian universe no more confirms the rigid diagrams of historical materialism than it does a cyclic theory.

When, however, Marx separated from the Hegelians of the right, this did not mean, said Engels, that Hegel was simply set aside. On the contrary, his insight into process was inserted into that new materialism which Feuerbach heralded. For Feuerbach, described by Engels as the link between Hegelianism and Marxism, helped sink the second of the two massive piles on which the communist ontology rests. His revolution was summed up concisely: Hegel's Absolute Idea is the fantastic survival of belief in a divine Creator. Actually, "the material, sensuously perceptible world to which we ourselves belong is the only reality. . . . Matter is not a product of mind, but mind itself is merely the highest product of matter."[12] Feuerbach is to be praised for his insistence on starting, not with thought, but with nonmental reality, not with the Idea, but with man. As Marx and Engels put it in *The German Ideology:* "Life is not determined by consciousness, but consciousness by life."

Still, even Feuerbach had his faults. For one thing, his materialism was too mechanistic and besides, he really only supplanted the old creeds with his new cult of abstract man. He was particularly unhappy in his failure to appreciate the values in

---

[12] Engels, "Ludwig Feuerbach," in Marx, *Selected Works,* Vol. 1, p. 435. See Marx, *Capital,* Vol. 1, p. 25: "The ideal is nothing else than the material world reflected by the human mind."

Hegelianism. One day in the British Museum, Marx was incensed by uncovering in the catalogues a reference to Dühring as a great thinker who had refuted Hegel. "The gentlemen in Germany (all except the theological reactionaries) think Hegel's dialectic is a 'dead horse,' " he wrote to Engels. "Feuerbach has much to answer for in this respect."[13] More than twenty years earlier, in the first of the theses jotted down at Brussels in the spring of 1845, Marx had criticized the chief defect of all materialisms so far, Feuerbach's included. They left to idealism the development of the active side of reality, human, sensuous activity, practice. The famous solution was to put together the Hegelian accent on becoming and the Feuerbachian materialism to produce a dialectical materialism which equated reality with a material universe profoundly implicated in change. This change was not to be understood as linear, but as following the dialectical pattern set up by a tension between what is and what is not, a tension resolved in a synthesis overcoming the conflict and speeding the world further along.

Persuaded as he was that the dialectical laws express the very dynamics of nature, Marx could logically have expected to find them verified in the story of man, which is, after all, only a phase of the total cosmic process. Find them he did, as the communist *Manifesto* was to announce in many tongues. It was the discovery of historical materialism; or rather, said Lenin, it was the consistent extension of materialism to the domain of social phenomena. It was a discovery which also owed something to the enthusiasm for labor which Marx's friendship with the Parisian communists had heightened. For this theory makes man's demiurgic function central. Men live because they work. On the one side, labor relates them to the infrahuman world in an interaction, which, ideally at least, ought to be a harmonious

---

[13] Marx to Engels, January 11, 1868, in Marx and Engels, *Selected Correspondence*, p. 233.

partnership simultaneously naturalizing men and humanizing nature. On the other side, it is because he works that a man finds himself involved in social, that is to say, cooperative, relationships. Language, consciousness, freedom—all these are social products which emerge when men come together for the sake of supporting their lives through united labor. These links between work, personal development, and community evolution are so fundamental that the individual hunter or fisher who forms the starting point for Smith and Ricardo belongs, says Marx bitingly, "to the insipid illusions of the eighteenth century . . . Robinsonades . . . fiction," like Rousseau's social contract. The fact is: "Man is in the most literal sense of the word a *zoon politikon,* not only a social animal, but an animal which can develop into an individual only in society."[14] Or, as the sixth thesis on Feuerbach put it: "The human essence is no abstraction inherent in each individual. In its reality it is the ensemble of social relations."

In the preface which Marx wrote for his study, *A Contribution to the Critique of Political Economy,* there is the classic text which summarizes this famous theory, this thread which guided its author through all the mazes of his research. The doctrine which maintains that the dialectical march of events in the economic order is the key to all the rest of human achievement may be reduced to two main points. First, the ideas and ideals, the art, religion, and philosophy, of any historical period are fundamentally intelligible in terms of the economic conditions of the era and the social and political forms which those economic factors have determined. Second, the engine of history

---

[14] Karl Marx, *A Contribution to the Critique of Political Economy,* translated by N. I. Stone, p. 268 (New York: International Library Publishing Company, 1904). The similarity of this position to the sort of "social behaviorism" associated in this country with such names as that of G. H. Mead is pointed out by Vernon Venable in his *Human Nature: The Marxian View,* p. 22 (New York: Alfred A. Knopf, 1945).

thus far has been the dialectical conflict of social classes necessarily created by the tension engendered by property relationships. Marx himself did not claim to have discovered the class conflict—bourgeois historians, he said, had often described it—but rather to have proved its economic source and its inevitable culmination, first in the dictatorship of the proletariat and finally in the flowering of a classless society.

Acceptance of this future dictatorship of the proletariat is, said Lenin, the kernel of Marxist theory, but two other aspects are more interesting for educators: the insistence on labor as the primal human activity and the belief that the whole stock of ideas ostensibly unrelated to the life of work is, nonetheless, ultimately a projection mirroring the facts of the economic order. "The religious world," to cite a single instance from the first volume of *Capital,* "is but the reflex of the real world." And to illustrate the point Marx argues that Christianity, especially in its bourgeois forms of Protestantism and deism, is a suitable religion for a capitalist society. For Christianity, he thinks, is also a cult of abstract man and thus nicely attuned to an economic set-up in which labor is regarded as a commodity quite divorced from the men whose action it is.

Engels sometimes tempered this theory when writing to friends in a private mood. He once remarked that religion and philosophy contain a good deal of "bunk" derived from the primitive's animistic notions, but that such conceptions have, for the most part, only a negative economic base. In a rudimentary economy where science is nearly nonexistent such magical fantasies fill the vacuum created by ignorance, but they evaporate when economic pressures force development of the scientific mastery of the world.[15] But it is still true that for Marxism essential man is man-the-worker whose ideological edifices rise and

---

[15] Engels to Schmidt, October 27, 1890, in Marx and Engels, *Selected Correspondence,* p. 482.

fall to the tempo of change in their economic foundation. The place of labor at the heart of the Marxian anthropology is, then, sufficiently evident, and it will be worthwhile to turn for a moment to some of Marx's comments on the nature of work itself and on the way nineteenth-century industrialism inhibited it, for these points, too, have their educational relevance.

LABOR AND THE MAKING AND DISMEMBERING OF MAN

Work is a concrete instance of the dialectic process. It might be viewed simply as a particular manifestation of the evolutionary flux in nature or as the dynamo of that history which makes men human. For although man, as *Capital* remarks, is one of nature's own forces, still all is not gray uniformity and motionless silence within that material continuum. On the contrary, men constantly interact with material nature, and these two powers are set against one another in the labor process. But besides illustrating this tension, human work is also the motion which overcomes it in a higher synthesis. Men act upon the wealth of the world—fish in the streams, timber in the forest, raw materials already filtered through previous labor. The work product itself resolves the conflict, for it is compounded of something of man and something of nature. "The process disappears in the product. . . . Labour has incorporated itself with its subject . . . the blacksmith forges and the product is a forging."[16]

But the analysis of work cannot stop here. After all, the simple friction involved in walking means some opposition between human and nonhuman forces, and breathing and eating also illustrate the exchange of materials. Besides, certain brute activities are curiously like man's labor—the instinctive building of dams and nests, webs and hives; the gathering of nuts and fruits. Exclusively human labor, as Marx labels it, is not necessarily specified by the superior technical excellence of the product.

---

[16] Marx, *Capital*, Vol. 1, p. 198.

Spiders and bees work with a delicacy and mastery that not many men can match. But man's work differs from purely instinctive operations because the work product is conceived in thought before it is attained in actuality. The goal of labor is forecast in the intentional order before it is achieved in the real order. "What distinguishes the worst architect from the best of bees is this, that the architect raises his structure in imagination before he erects it in reality."[17] Though the philosophical perspective is so different, the conclusion here is very like that of St. Thomas discussing exemplary causality. For the scholastic doctor observes that in some agents the *form* of the thing to be made pre-exists "according to intelligible being, as in those that act by their intellect; and thus the likeness of a house pre-exists in the mind of a builder."[18]

Labor has, too, a utilitarian or instrumental aspect which distinguishes it from play's production for the sake of activity or art's production for the arrest of beauty. For all work, intellectual as well as manual, contributes to the necessary provision of the means of subsistence. Work has conditions to impose for the sake of the values sought. There is, for instance, the law of the material itself, to which Marx does not advert explicitly since it is fairly obvious. Any worker is bound by the limitations of the stuff he manipulates. He can irrigate his garden with a stream but he cannot carve a bench from it. There is the law of economic necessity, for the human race as a collective must work even though individuals may idle. Finally, there is the law imposed upon the worker by his own purpose. Often it may be a hard law which requires sustained concentration when the goal is long-range. But in fulfilling the conditions laid down by his own objective the worker is also fulfilling himself. The product

---

[17] *Ibid.*

[18] St. Thomas Aquinas, *The Summa Theologica of St. Thomas Aquinas,* translated by Fathers of the English Dominican Province, Vol. 1, p. 87. New York: Benziger Brothers, 1947.

he creates embodies both his vision and his desire, and the work process itself actualizes physical and psychical virtualities. But if the attainment of a self-appointed aim is a self-realization, there is also room for rub here when workers are never free to set their own goals.

If labor is a prime factor in the development both of societies and persons, then the more varied and satisfying a man's work, the more richly will his capacities be actualized. If the great types are, let us say, the painter, the plumber, and the pastry cook, then to become all of these, so far as possible, is to become more fully human. In the communist society one might even be a philosopher or poet—after hours. Still, some division or distribution of work has always been necessary; it is a simple corollary of the cooperative nature of human labor. Yet it is also true, said Marx, that such division involves some crippling of mind and body. In the bourgeois society, however, which boomed in nineteenth-century Europe, Marx believed this whole business had been carried to a pathological extreme by industrial manufacture. Once upon a time European farmers were also spinners and weavers. But now the march of technology had separated agriculture from manufacturing, while the machine divided the spinner in England from the weaver in India. Man himself was dismembered.

The feudal regime had plenty of faults, Marx thought, but at least the independent peasant or artisan personally exercised some knowledge, judgment, and will. "These faculties are now required only for the workshop as a whole." The pieceworker who spends his life endlessly repeating one limited and routine operation has become a "crippled monstrosity." He has been wounded at the very roots of his life.[19] But such a dehumanizing division of labor is only possible, Marx innocently supposed, in a class-divided, capitalist society where the bourgeois masters of

---

[19] Marx, *Capital*, Vol. 1, pp. 396, 399.

resource can compel each worker to his monotonous task. The collective laborer, the proletariat, has reached a new peak of social productive power, but the atomization of production itself has come to the point where the individual's role is not only impoverishing but positively pernicious. At the same time, it is impossible for men to break from these cadres because capitalist society has made them rigid. The children of the factory hand have only the factory to look forward to.

It is never the advance of technology that Marx deplores but only what he conceives to be its misuse by entrepreneurs. In a speech delivered in 1856 at the anniversary celebration of the Chartist *People's Paper* he summed up his view of the whole nineteenth-century epoch: "In our days everything seems pregnant with its contrary; machinery gifted with the wonderful power of shortening and fructifying human labour, we behold starving and overworking it. . . . At the same pace that mankind masters nature, man seems to become enslaved to other men or to his own infamy. . . . All our invention and progress seem to result in endowing material forces with intellectual life, and in stultifying human life into a material force."[20]

Capital's pages burn with concrete illustrations: soot-covered young girls working with the men on pit banks and coke heaps all night long; nine-year-old boys doing three successive twelve-hour shifts in the rolling mills and sleeping on the furnace floor with a jacket for coverlid; wives and children of the Irish peasantry hired to feed the rollers of scutching mills and suffering appalling accidents, limbs torn from the trunk, because factories were not equipped with even the simplest safety devices. In olden times, Marx once said in a burst of bitter rhetoric, this horror of child murder was limited to the occasional secret rites

---

[20] Karl Marx, "Speech at the Anniversary of the 'People's Paper,'" in Marx, *Selected Works*, Vol. 2, pp. 427-28. This critique of industrialism parallels in places the indictments later drawn up by Leo XIII and Pius XI.

of Moloch and Moloch, at least, showed no special preference for the children of the poor.

All this means that the individual worker is estranged from his very self. He has sold his labor to the industrialist and thereby alienated his basic activity. His work is concretized in objects he does not enjoy and so he is alienated from nature. It is governed by goals he does not set; inhumanly constricted in its range, and so it leaves him in profound interior division. Moreover, he is alienated from his species; a stranger to himself and hence to all others—something that could not happen if, besides cooperating in industry, the workers collectively owned the means of production and reaped its benefits.

This is the black side. But in the east there is already showing the first glimmer of the light which will dissolve the darkness. The dialectical movement of history operates inexorably. The present condition itself of economic life stirs the insistent demand for integration and abolition of the alienations. It is communist society which will accomplish this, once the proletarians have subjected the forces of production to themselves as a collective. Industry will be thoroughly regulated then. No one will greedily appropriate surplus values and the estrangement of men from the results of their work will be healed. Moreover, in this society work will achieve its full humanizing power, for no one need confine himself to a single sphere, "but each can become accomplished in any branch he wishes, society regulates the general production and thus makes it possible for me to do one thing today and another tomorrow, to hunt in the morning, fish in the afternoon, rear cattle in the evening, criticize after dinner, just as I have a mind, without ever becoming hunter, fisherman, shepherd or critic."[21]

This new day has not yet dawned, however—not even in Russia, we hear. Its educational practice cannot therefore be de-

---

[21] Marx and Engels, *German Ideology*, p. 22.

scribed, but perhaps one can rough in its probable outlines. Doubtless Marx himself would not be fond of such business, for he once remarked that in social problems theory alone does not get a flea-hop nearer the solution. Nonetheless, he was fond of theorizing, and it is possible to draw out the implication of those conclusions which he supposed himself to have grounded on a scientific survey of facts.

"THE GERM OF THE EDUCATION OF THE FUTURE"

Some of the characteristic themes of Marxism serve very neatly as the ground plan of a philosophy of education. There is, for instance, its genuine, if limited, humanistic concern for the welfare and maturation of men. There is its sense of history and the link it forges between the processes of society's historical development and the personal development of individuals. Such historical awareness is needed in those who must safeguard the continuity of society by helping the young possess themselves of the cultural deposit. And though one must quarrel with the way Marx read the record, it cannot be denied that he was aware of the importance of the historical context and saw human problems unrolling as moments of an epochal drama in time. For him, indeed, men were not merely developed in this sequential process and under its influences, but the physical and social environments were the real generators, not merely the soil and food, of the authentically human. Since Marx realized, at least to some extent, that the individual is humanized by his social involvements, he was able to integrate personal and social expansion—although, of course, only on his own terms. In *Capital* he argues that the constant search for technical efficiency in modern industry itself nourishes the revolutionary spirit because it highlights the fact of change and thereby compels men to acknowledge the significance of this fact in their own lives.

Nevertheless even those who are in general agreement with the Marxian anthropology would hardly consider it a fully rounded statement. Problems of personality, for example, are scarcely touched upon. This is natural enough considering the demands of Marx's economic research and the polemical tone of his philosophical writings. But those who disagree with his basic antitheistic postulate will regard his view of man, not merely as sketchy, but as irremediably atrophied; intrinsically truncated and compromised by the supremacy of the collectivity in communist theory. The penetrating Russian religious thinker Berdyaev concluded that Marx had no real philosophy of human personality for two reasons. First, because the denial of the nonmaterial factor in the human composite has, in effect, established the primacy of the generic being in man over his personal being. Second, because Marx's futurism makes the men of today merely means with a view to the man of tomorrow, and so diminishes the intrinsic worth of each individual. Certainly Marxism does place the problem of society ahead of the problem of man, if for no other reason than that it sees the human problem as really a social one. Before Marx's death, however, there was born in Freud an investigator who would return to the study of the individual psyche which, howsoever much conditioned by society and its various disorders, remains a question in its own right and one that really escapes the simplist explanations of any materialism, including Freud's own.

Marx and Engels had nothing very constructive to say about the improvement of the schools they saw around them. After all, their eyes were on the mounting wave of the future which would soon engulf all contemporary forms. At the same time, their futuristic and "scientific" theory disinclined them to attempt descriptions of education in that new world. It would inevitably be, anyhow, what the revolutionary forces made it, and one should scorn utopian dreamers like Dühring who thought they could manipulate current institutions for the realization of their own social blueprints. But from the few pages that are devoted to education and from the general principles of the system it is possible for one to get some notion of what Marx and Engels expected in the schools of the future.

So far as education in the broad sense is concerned, the informal education given by social life itself, the communist society of the future will be an ideal agency since it will open to all the full humanizing force of work. Consequently the classic practical recommendation of Marxism applies here: Work for the revolution! It is quite true, say Marx and Engels from their nineteenth-century lookout, that the conflict between *bourgeoisie* and dispossessed is moving to an inevitable climax. But although the event is surely coming, it will actually arrive, or arrive more speedily, through the activity of the revolutionaries. Educators ought not, therefore, fritter away their energies on senseless little schemes. No amount of adjustment of the present institutions is possible or desirable: not possible because the dynamism of history is moving toward the abolition, not the purification of class society; not desirable because so long as there are any divisions, some men will be cut off from the sources of growth. Work instead for the inception of communist society. "Not criticism but revolution is the driving force of history," said *The German Ideology*. One must expect first that transitional period during which capitalism crumbles as the state withers away and the proletariat dictate. But once the plenary communist society has arrived, three changes of great educational import will have been accomplished. All the old, crippling ideologies will have been swept out; full contact with the humanizing resources of work will be restored to everybody; and each man can lay hold of the whole range of work products in the arts, science, and technological conveniences.

At one point in *Capital* Marx observed that, since Engels and others had adequately pictured the moral degradation of the working classes, he would himself call attention rather to "the intellectual desolation, artificially produced by converting immature human beings into mere machines for the fabrication

of surplus value, a state of mind clearly distinguishable from
the natural ignorance which keeps the mind fallow without de-
stroying its capacity for development."[22] This situation had become so inflamed that industry was forced to recognize that
variation of work and a broad development of a man's technical
skills are actually fundamental laws of production. Consequently some technical and agricultural schools were started to
provide child workers with at least the rudiments of learning.[23]
But these provisions, Marx wrote, though better than nothing,
were still hopelessly inadequate if contrasted with the promise
of communist society.

In that society the technological genius of industrial civilization would not be scrapped, but its cornucopia would be
emptied for all, since the proletariat would have collectively
appropriated factories and farms. By erasure of the bourgeois
ruling classes men would have rid themselves of those inhibiting
customs which reflected the former property relationships and
bolstered the position of the wealthy elite. That group, for instance, had fostered a sham distinction between intellectual and
manual work which was much to their own interest. They liked
the dichotomy between themselves as active ideologists who
planned life for the rest and a passive multitude whose business
it would be to labor in docility. Marx was confident that communism would dissolve all such class distinctions and cure the alienations that they were presumed to have produced. The change
would be gradual, certainly. Common ownership of the means
of production would not be accompanied immediately by a distribution of products solely on the basis of need. For a while it
would be necessary to follow the crass norm which rewards
equally an equal amount of work. But when the "higher plane
of communist society" is reached, work will be so interesting
and the human fellowship enveloping it so strong that everyone

---

[22] Marx, *Capital*, Vol. 1, p. 436.   [23] *Ibid.*, p. 534.

will work joyfully, inspired purely by the intrinsic values of labor and the desire to see "the springs of cooperative wealth flow more abundantly." Then can "Society inscribe on its banners: from each according to his ability, to each according to his needs."[24]

At this point the activity of each man will really coincide with the conditions of material life, for all will be owners and all will be consumers according to their needs. Everyone will be united with his own work, since he will personally reap its fruits as part of the collective which plans, owns, and operates the machinery of life production. There will be no need for religion or idealism, since the society from its economic base up will reflect the satisfying integrity and dignity of the true ideal, communism's new man.

Such a society will itself be the best of all schools, for in it men will at last adequately realize their industrial potential and thereby become genuinely human. Abolition of classes will mean abolition of that warping division of labor which condemns a man to a lifetime of screwing in bolts or making pinheads. In the new order, said *The German Ideology*, matters will be so planned that "nobody has one exclusive sphere of activity but each man can become accomplished in any branch he wishes." To effect this, new types of social organization will emerge. For example, domestic society as we know it will disappear and in the workers' collective a higher familial form will take shape. It is true that in modern industry, where workers are not owners but victims of exploitation, the association of the sexes is "pestiferous." But in the communist world "the fact of the collective working group being composed of individuals of both sexes and all ages must necessarily, under suitable conditions, become a source of humane development."[25] Since none

---

[24] Marx, *Selected Works*, Vol. 2, pp. 564-66.
[25] Marx, *Capital*, Vol. 1, p. 536.

will be exempted from the obligation to work, social unity will be firm and all-inclusive. Sensible hours and rational working conditions will make labor delightful. Enjoying their work, people will help one another and community spirit will be strong and pure. As a means of developing an all-round dexterity and of abolishing the existing dualism of town and country, agricultural and manufacturing industries will be combined, populations will be redistributed, and industrial and farming armies will be formed.

All these procedures will coalesce to create for everyone that variety of work experience which is the fundamental humanizing factor. Still, Marx and Engels did not think of work as the only worthwhile experience. In their new dispensation, therefore, the satisfactions of science and the arts are to be universally accessible. But this itself only means bringing all men into full touch with the material and intellectual production of the whole world. The richness of a personality depends upon the depth and variety of a man's relationships to this world. For the oppressed worker the environment is hardly more significant than it is for a beast—a place of bare forage and refuge. Yet a man really produces, said Marx, only when he is free of these physical needs and can create in beauty. It was his fond hope that communism would liberate man for a fruitful communication with the cosmos in all its richness and that this work dialogue would in turn bring to peak his full range of powers for action and enjoyment.

Formal education in this utopia is clear enough in outline if not in detail. Its over-all goal would be development of the ideal good man according to Marxist specifications. Such a man will be formed through interaction with the resources of his environment—man-made as well as natural. Perhaps everyone can hope to relish, as Marx and Engels did, the genius of Dante and Darwin; the disparate "products" of Cervantes, Watt, and Mozart; cigars, smoked herring, and fox hunting. But this will only be possible in a society which assigns to work its rightful primacy. Accordingly the only acceptable education will combine labor with instruction and gymnastics. It will be an education in the exclusive charge of the communist society itself—all the children in the free public schools, said the *Manifesto*. The capitalists will yelp, it admits, and engage in bourgeois claptrap about the family and education. They will say that communism destroys the most hallowed of relations when it transfers control of education from the home to civil society. But, the *Manifesto* retorts, the communists want only to rescue the schools from their present control by this same *bourgeoisie*. And until they have done so, Marx advised in the *Critique of the Gotha Program,* neither the Church nor the state, that tool of capitalism, should have any influence on education.

Both in that *Critique* and in *Capital*, Marx had a few fragmentary observations to make on the curricula of the schools in the future. They should include, he wrote, at least elementary instruction for everyone and technical training, both theoretical and practical. The whole program proposed vaguely for "every child over a certain age," has the three distinct aspects noted above: formal classroom work, physical training through gymnastics with the addition of drill for boys, and productive labor in agriculture and industry. So far as the actual school hours are concerned, neither Marx nor Engels has anything definite or original to propose, although one may conclude that the language study so esteemed by them both would have an important place. Quite in the vein of a contemporary defender of "liberal learning" Engels wrote in his chastisement of Dühring:

> He wants also to do away with the two levers which in the world as it is today give at least the opportunity of rising above the narrow national standpoint: knowledge of the ancient languages, which opens a wider common horizon at least to those who have had a classical education; and knowledge of modern languages, through the medium of which alone the people of different nations

can make themselves understood by one another and acquaint themselves with what is happening beyond their own frontiers.[26]

Science and technology would also surely be dominant. It was just such an accent, in fact, that Soviet Russia later incarnated in its polytechnical institutes designed for basic training in a variety of industrial skills. In April 1958, Premier Khrushchev gave voice to this same emphasis when he told the thirteenth Komsomol Congress that Soviet schools must prepare thoroughly educated people equipped with a basic scientific formation as well as with the capacity and the desire for a life of systematic productive labor. So far as Marx was concerned, moreover, the work part of the school program should mean real work. A general prohibition of child labor is not at all desirable, he wrote in the *Critique of the Gotha Program*. It would, for one thing, be reactionary, since as long as hours are strictly regulated and safety measures insured, "an early combination of productive labor with education is one of the most potent means for the transformation of present day society."[27] Besides, the idea is psychologically sound. Marx apparently adopted the opinion of certain English factory inspectors who were convinced that children learned more on a diet of half a day at labor and half at school than they did if kept in the classrooms all day long.

The logic of Marxism, to be sure, forbids its architects to plan the educational program of the future in much more fixed detail. The very flowing character of reality must discourage such a venture. "All successive historical situations," wrote Engels in *Ludwig Feuerbach*, "are only transitory stages in the endless course of development of human society from the lower to the higher. . . . Dialectical philosophy dissolves all concep-

---

[26] Engels, *Dühring*, p. 358.
[27] Marx, *Selected Works*, Vol. 2, p. 583. See also Marx, *Capital*, Vol. 1, p. 529 for the opinion of the English factory inspectors.

tions of final and absolute truth and of a final absolute state of humanity corresponding to it."[28]

Nevertheless this much is firmly asserted: mankind will escape out of the realm of necessity into the realm of freedom when the revolution transforms work from a mere means of subsistence into the prime necessity of life at its best. Then indeed, according to the dream of Marx and Engels, men will enter into the plenitude of their humanity as they enter into the plenitude of their labor. They will have become the true masters of the universe—of nature, of history, of society, and of themselves.

---

[28] Marx, *Selected Works*, Vol. 1, pp. 421-22.

Dewey's Theory
of Work in Education

According to Albert P. Pinkevitch, one of the first Soviet educational theorists, John Dewey was only a talented bourgeois. Nevertheless Pinkevitch had a genial regard for him because, almost alone among philosophers, Dewey gave manual work a place of honor in the school. Although he rejected Marxism's exaggerated claims for labor as the decisive fashioner of human life, Dewey wove work activity directly into the program of elementary instruction and defended its place there with a coherence and subtlety that make Marx's pedagogical observations seem shallow. The theory supporting Dewey's recommendations has little in common either with caricatures of progressive education or with direct vocational training. He had no fondness for an uproar of busy work or a jovial hurly-burly of basketmaking and clay modeling aimed at keeping little children happy and harmlessly occupied. His good sense also rejected schemes for explicit job preparation in that elementary school which was his special concern. Even when such training did begin, Dewey thought it ought to be—to use his own terms—less an apprenticeship than a laboratory for insights into the intellectual foundation, the general methods, and the humanistic values of work. Mastery of technical skills, whether they be those of a doctor, lawyer, teacher, or mechanic, would be best left to the job itself.

True to this spirit, Dewey's generalized humanism of work is itself an application of the laboratory idea as distinct from the apprentice idea.[1]

It is an application firmly anchored in his philosophical analyses of intelligence and morality. As a man, Dewey's lifelong preoccupation was humanitarian, but as a philosopher his perennial problem was epistemological. These two interests, however, were closely linked, for he saw human intelligence precisely as the supreme tool for constructing a progressively richer and nobler life, and he preferred to talk of "good" or "bad" thinking rather than "true" or "false." A moralistic tone of this sort was quite reasonable in one for whom the main business of thought is "control of the environment in behalf of human progress and well-being, the effort at control being stimulated by the needs, the defects, the troubles, which accrue when the environment coerces and suppresses man or when man endeavors in ignorance to override the environment."[2] This accent on the ethical and pragmatic benefits of intelligence is the clue, in turn, to such activities as the textile project in the University of Chicago's laboratory school which Dewey founded and then immortalized in *The School and Society*. When the children there set themselves to carding wool and ginning cotton, spin-

---

[1] John Dewey, "The Relation of Theory to Practice in Education," in *The Relation of Theory to Practice in the Education of Teachers*, Third Yearbook of the National Society for the Scientific Study of Education, Part 1, p. 10 (Chicago: The University of Chicago Press, 1904). Vocational training, says Dewey here, should supply the intellectual method and material of good workmanship instead of trying to make on the spot an efficient workman. Even this "laboratory" approach will result to some extent in forming an efficient workman. It is simply a question of how best to use the limited time available to the school. "Relatively speaking, the wise employ of this short time is in laying scientific foundations. These cannot be adequately secured when one is doing the actual work of the profession, while professional life does afford time for acquiring and perfecting skill of the more technical sort" (*ibid.*, p. 11).

[2] John Dewey, *Essays in Experimental Logic*, p. 22. Chicago: The University of Chicago Press, 1916.

ning and weaving, cutting and sewing, this was not because of
some cultural-epoch theory (although occasionally Dewey did
speak of recapitulating historic developments), but it was rather
intended as an initiation into the best employment of intelligence itself and as activity leading into the method of specifically human excellence.

Theses of this sort are proved, in Dewey's opinion, if man
is surveyed from the standpoint of the experimental sciences
which best reveal him for what he really is. Biology shows us
an organism in a natural matrix; sociology and psychology, an
individual in the social matrix: and in either case we observe a
living being ceaselessly interacting with its environment and di-
recting all its efforts toward the prolongation and expansion of
life. Man is genetically continuous with the nonhuman, material
universe—nature, that whole of which he is one part. It is a
serial and processive whole, endlessly varied, ongoing, often unpredictable, rewarding as well as perilous; and even its apparently stable elements are only partially so, for the total sum of
reality is always evolving.

"To exist," said Dewey once, "is to be in process, in
change."[3] A human life is a history of events and the events are
moments in the conversation and commerce of men with dynamic nature. The primary categories of this life are those of
success and failure in that rhythmic process. But success is no
matter of chance. It is the product of men's manipulation and
reorganization of the factors in their present situation so as to
insure better outcomes tomorrow. For "we live forward," and
our current experience is itself "a future implicated in a present." This conscious control of the flowing stuff of life for pre-

---

[3] John Dewey, "What I Believe," *Forum* 83:178, March 1930. In the course of his
lifetime Dewey published a number of philosophical creeds. For a similar
statement of principles, written however with special reference to the school,
see John Dewey, "My Pedagogic Creed," *Journal of the National Education
Association* 18:291-95, December 1929.

dicted results *is* mind, for "mind is primarily a verb," and ideas are plans of operations to be performed.[4]

But human work, as Dewey understood it, is really the primary manifestation of this productive and instrumental activity of intelligence. It is, to begin with, a response to the problematic elements of existence, for surely there is no problem more insistent than that of preserving life itself. It was in their work, then, that men first used the genuinely fecund method of inquiry, the practical method of hypothesis and test. The farmer had a field to sow, the carpenter a bench to make; and each was forced to visualize his goal in relation to the means for reaching it. Their strategy was devised in light of the total situation; and if the corn grew or the bench weathered hard usage, those experiences confirmed or corrected the initial forecasts. Here was the "scientific method" in an unreflective but authentic form, and the sciences themselves, said Dewey, gradually unfolded from just such useful social occupations.

That social note, moreover, deserves an additional emphasis, for it was associative living which provided the essential nurture, the motive, and the setting for the farmer and the artisan. It was the funded social experience available in their community which educated them in the skills of their crafts. It was the cooperative division of labor which made it possible for one man to plow while another hammered and each profited from his neighbor's achievements. Finally, it was loyalty to the demands of their common life and interest in its possible improvement which made them "good" men, men of social competence.

---

[4] See John Dewey and others, *Creative Intelligence*, pp. 12-13 (New York: Henry Holt and Company, 1917); John Dewey, *Art as Experience*, p. 263 (New York: Minton, Balch and Company, 1934): "Mind is primarily a verb. It denotes all the ways in which we deal consciously and expressly with the situations in which we find ourselves"; John Dewey, *The Quest for Certainty: A Study of the Relation of Knowledge and Action*, p. 138 (New York: Minton, Balch and Company, 1929).

Work, in short, besides introducing men to logical method also involves them in those basic social enterprises which alone form sound moral character.

Science has generalized and refined this pragmatic method of work, but little children are not capable of coping adequately with the subtleties of modern physical theory. Yet they do have, said Dewey in *The School and Society,* a natural bent toward activity and a spontaneous interest in the social occupations they observe in the adult world. He hoped to exploit the educational possibilities of that interest by providing school opportunities for work projects which should serve as a vital induction into the best humanistic resource—that instrumental method of work and science which in its cooperative aspect is also the method of genuine ethical training. All this deserves to be set forth in somewhat greater detail and within the context of Dewey's own life. Nevertheless the core of this theory is summarized in a single sentence from *Democracy and Education:* "The problem of the educator is to engage pupils in these activities in such ways that while manual skill and technical efficiency are gained and immediate satisfaction found in the work, together with preparation for later usefulness, these things shall be subordinated to *education*—that is, to intellectual results and the forming of a socialized disposition."[5]

QUESTING FOR FAITH IN THE WILDERNESS

He did not expect, John Dewey once wrote, to see a genuine integration of knowledge achieved in his own lifetime. Nevertheless he added: "A mind that is not too egotistically impatient can have faith that this unification will issue in its season."[6] He

---

[5] John Dewey, *Democracy and Education*, p. 231. New York: The Macmillan Company, 1916.

[6] John Dewey, "From Absolutism to Experimentalism," in George P. Adams and William Pepperell Montague, editors, *Contemporary American Philosophy*, Vol. 2, p. 26. New York: The Macmillan Company, 1930.

was conscious, no doubt, that his own philosophy was not the desired synthesis; and indeed it does contain a number of theses which are incongruous if not mutually contradictory. If one attends, however, to the dominant ideals which claimed Dewey's allegiance—his mystique, so to speak—there will be discovered in his thought a general unity, real and persistent, even though particular contradictions remain undissolved. In the face of criticism he maintained no more than this himself. "Inconsistencies and shifts have taken place; the most I can claim is that I have moved fairly steadily in one direction."[7]

On this pilgrimage the philosophical traveler was buoyed up by a vivid sense of the bounty of life, his inspiration was an unshakable faith in its resources as themselves "the sole ultimate authority," and his goal was a secularized city of the future in which this faith should become substance. Dewey was the staunchest believer in that new common faith he preached: "Devotion, so intense as to be religious, to intelligence as a force in social action." Quite possibly he found it, at times, a strenuous business. It was always compelling him, he said, to view reality *sub specie generationis* and to reject the dangerous allure of the old ideal of contemplation *sub specie aeternitatis*. Yet "there are moments," he once wrote, "when the demand for peace, to be left alone and relieved from the continual claim of the world in which we live that we be up and doing something about it, seems irresistible; when the responsibilities imposed by living in a moving universe seem intolerable."[8] But he could

---

[7] John Dewey, "Experience, Knowledge and Value: A Rejoinder," in Paul Arthur Schilpp, editor, *The Philosophy of John Dewey*, p. 520 (Evanston: Northwestern University, 1939). A succinct discussion of some of the oppositions in Dewey's philosophy is provided by William Taft Feldman, *The Philosophy of John Dewey: A Critical Analysis*, pp. 114-23 (Baltimore: The Johns Hopkins Press, 1934).

[8] John Dewey, *Philosophy and Civilization*, p. 54 (New York: Minton, Balch and Company, 1931). The comment on life's experiences as "sole ultimate authority" will be found in Dewey's essay, "What I Believe," p. 176.

bestir himself with the thought that, even if philosophy did no more than clear roadblocks from the pathway to the future, still this is something. "Forty years spent in wandering in a wilderness like that of the present is not a sad fate—unless one attempts to make himself believe that the wilderness is after all itself the promised land."[9] Dewey seemed never to have lost confidence that the wilderness would flower if men once directed their energies toward application of the scientific method to social problems and suffused this effort with the ardor formerly reserved for religious practices. He could at least claim that his trust in the "office of intelligence as a continuously reconstructive agency" was an honest index of his own life and career.

That life casts considerable light on Dewey's thought, since on his own admission the events of his personal history had peculiar significance for his philosophy. What books had given him was only technical, he said, compared with what persons and situations had taught him and what he had been forced to puzzle about because of some problem in which he had found himself entangled during the course of his life. It was an enormously long life, for he was in his ninety-third year when he died in 1952, and so astonishingly successful and productive as to be quite unparalleled from the point of view of temporal felicity by any other career in the annals of philosophy. For this reason it also contrasted sharply with one of the more conventional patterns in the story of American intellectual and artistic

---

[9] Dewey, in Adams and Montague, *Contemporary American Philosophy*, Vol. 2, pp. 26-27. This essay is Dewey's own brief account of his intellectual history. It shares interest with the sketch, "Biography of John Dewey," which introduces the volume edited by Schilpp, *The Philosophy of John Dewey*. For this sketch was written by Dewey's daughters from material supplied by him, and a note subjoined to it declares: "In the emphasis on various influences and in the philosophical portions it may be regarded as an autobiography, but its subject is not responsible for the form nor for all the details" (Schilpp, *The Philosophy of John Dewey*, p. 3). Details here of Dewey's life are taken from these sources.

genius. This is the pattern which calls for eccentricity, illness, or untimely death, for unrequited struggle, frustration, or defeat, and which has been modeled in one or other style by Emily Dickinson and Thoreau in their respective hermitages; by Veblen and Peirce as cranky square pegs in an academic world where all the holes were round; by rebels and uneasy geniuses of every sort—Mark Twain, Henry George, Hawthorne, Melville, Poe, Wolfe. Even the magnificent William James, for all his humanity and brilliance, had passages of darkness. But the case with Dewey, so far as our present knowledge goes, was wholly otherwise. No doubt he knew the ordinary pressures of human existence and in his youth, perhaps, some of the special ones reserved for men of great mental gifts. But these seemed simply to have characterized his life as human without staining it irrevocably and the total impression is that of a sun-flooded river moving with calm power over its lengthy course. As an obscure little country boy he spent the last winter of the Civil War in Virginia near his soldier father in a Union camp. His death nearly a century later was front-page news, for he had enjoyed universal acclaim for decades. He had poured out books and articles; held distinguished academic posts and engaged in social, political, and educational enterprises at home and abroad. His domestic life was equally favored and those who knew him personally were enthusiastic about the man himself and about his kindness and affability—qualities not always so evident when he was sizing up other philosophies.

The golden amplitude of this great career is itself a key to Dewey's thought. It is hardly surprising, for instance, that a life so blessed should have produced a philosophy strongly optimistic in tone and free of that somber preoccupation with problems of destiny and evil so characteristic of many other thinkers from Socrates to Sartre. Whatever the cause, the optimistic tone is real enough and enhanced by a style which is sometimes turgid and polemical but for the most part serene, confident, and not

without a certain dignity and grace. The spirit of the late nineteenth century, of those secure, "deep, claret-colored years," as
Willa Cather once called them, breathes through such passages
as these from *Reconstruction in Philosophy:* "Growth itself is
the only moral 'end' . . . The problem of evil ceases to be a
theological and metaphysical one, and is perceived to be the
practical problem of reducing, alleviating, as far as may be
removing, the evils of life."[10] For Dewey these evils themselves
were only helpful stimuli to thought, blessings in disguise like
the grain of sand in the oyster's shell. Nowadays such hopeful
rationalism is apt to seem painfully unrealistic; but it is only
fair to notice that right down into the atomic age Dewey, round-
ing out three quarters of a century of philosophizing, kept his
own faith active and intact.

Between his life and his thought, however, there is another
parallelism more profound than this rather easy one between
his optimism and his good fortune. For just as his life itself was
unusually rich, so at the heart of his philosophy lies an intense,
correlative perception of the very wealth and mystery of human
existence. Everyone has this insight to some degree and perceives, however fitfully, that even the most routine career is
incredibly varied; has level upon level of significance and
realms of terror as well as those of ecstasy; teems with new possibilities for expansion and fresh experience; is now harsh and
now beneficent and never fully explored or possessed but always
problematic. In Dewey's thought there is an overmastering intuition of this kind, a deep appreciation of the resource that is
life itself. His concept of "experience," for example, is a crucial
and notably difficult one. Sometimes it stands for everything
the human organism undergoes as it interacts with its environment. Sometimes it seems limited to those events and interac-

---

[10] John Dewey, *Reconstruction in Philosophy*, p. 177. New York: Henry Holt and
Company, 1920.

tions of which we are conscious or whose meanings we have grasped. Sometimes, according to Richard McKeon, Dewey used it as synonym for the cultural context. But what always lies behind the term is that vivid awareness of the manifold reality which is human life.

The history of Dewey's speculation is quite naturally, then, the history of his search for the meaning of existence—and this despite his verbal denial of the very possibility of any such search. The quest concluded with some distinctive doctrines. The only method of sure inquiry, it maintained, is that of the physical sciences and the category of human life is adequately expressed in biological terms—hence, a biological naturalism. Intelligence, for instance, is a biological tool both for survival and new arrivals, since it is capable of creating values not found in the infrahuman world although not essentially different from it. In human conduct life itself is the ultimate judge against which there is no appeal; and the beginning of progress, we are told in *Human Nature and Conduct,* is "loyalty to whatever in the established environment makes a life of excellence possible"—although to say as much still leaves excellence itself rather undefined. When these theses are proposed in Dewey's unilateral and exclusive sense, not only Christians but many other philosophers find them unacceptable, although the critics will grant the zeal for wisdom which inspired their defender. Here, however, it is only necessary to note that, since the link between Dewey's educational theory and his general philosophy is organic, his views on work experience in the school unroll directly and clearly from certain relevant philosophical positions. These positions, in turn, may be profitably examined according to that genetic method which Dewey himself favored; that is to say, in their relationship to the philosopher's life, that soil from which they grew.

When Marx probed the abscesses of the European industrial economy and charged it with warping men by chaining them to monotonous work routines, he was aware that more humane conditions obtained elsewhere. In *Capital* he quotes the report of a Frenchman who had migrated to California firmly convinced that he was fit only for his trade of letterpress printing. But finding himself in a world of adventurers who changed, he said, their occupations as often as their shirt, he too became in rapid succession miner, typographer, slater, and plumber. And having discovered that he was fit for many sorts of work, he began to feel, by his own account, less of a mollusk and more of a man. It was in just this American society, whose frontiers were still open, that Dewey grew up. He was born in Burlington ten years after the Gold Rush and eight years before the first volume of *Capital* appeared. The Dewey family had even then been long resident in America and was very much "old stock" with a lineage ancient by American standards. The New England milieu in their locality was still relatively unsmudged by heavy industrialism, so that it preserved an aura of tradition without losing a sense of the future. It was likely soil for the nurture of a philosopher imbued with a deep *pietas* for the American Idea—as he conceived it. One is reminded of Hellas, where citizens prided themselves, not on wealth or leisure, but on ancestry traced back to the first inhabitants of Attica, sired by the local gods. And in fact, Sidney Hook relates a revealing incident. He writes: "During the days when the Hoovers and Mellons were riding high, and making invidious distinctions between types of Americans, and appealing to the American way of life as a bulwark against social change, he [Dewey] remarked, 'Where I was raised the Hoovers and Mellons would have had a hard time passing for Americans.' "[11]

But this stuffiness was not the whole story. Even then Vermont would have felt the spirit of the hour—one friendly to

---

[11] Sidney Hook, *John Dewey: An Intellectual Portrait*, p. 6. New York: John Day Company, 1939.

change, sanguine about the future, and uncertain about the stability of traditional values and beliefs. Besides, John Dewey did not stay in Vermont. Moreover, before he entered on the wider national scene, he had been plunged into the dark center of the great intellectual perplexity of modern times, the apparent conflict of religion and science as readers of reality. It was a true personal crisis, he reported. With his strong feeling for the mystery of human experience he could not but be conscious, as he wrote years later, of "a demand for unification that was doubtless an intense emotional craving, and yet was a hunger that only an intellectualized subject-matter could satisfy."[12] When at fifteen he entered the University of Vermont in his home town, he was looking, as he put it, for a system of thought that would nourish both his head and his heart. But what he encountered were two rival and extreme interpretations: a declining Protestant apologetic and the trumpeting scientism of Huxley and Comte. The religion he knew was, on the popular level, more emotional than theological and its academic defense was so intertwined with Scotch intuitionalism that the failure of the one meant the ruin of the other. Neither appealed to Dewey, but he was much impressed by a Huxley text in the physiology course and by a condensation of Comte's *Positive Philosophy*. The former exalted the method of physical science and the latter stimulated his dedication to the task of applying this method to social and ethical problems.

When he graduated in 1879, however, Dewey had not yet decisively reconciled this tension between religious belief and scientific challenge. He was still conscious of what he himself called an inward laceration, for his education thus far induced in him a feeling of isolation and internal division. Although the religion offered him was emotionally unsatisfactory because in-

---

[12] Dewey, in Adams and Montague, *Contemporary American Philosophy*, Vol. 2, p. 19.

tellectually inadequate, still this crisis never formed, he wrote, the material of a philosophical problem even though it caused personal suffering. This was partly due to his conviction that religion must follow after and adapt itself to one's rationally derived world view. It was also derived from his total commitment to the methodology of the natural sciences with its correlative exclusion, for lack of tools to handle them, of certain philosophical problems with religious import—the existence of God, the immortality of the soul, the validity of natural-law theory, the investigation of the credentials of Christianity. In his maturity Dewey evolved the notion that philosophy's business is not the establishment of beliefs and values anyhow, but rather the critical examination of those actually obtaining in the philosopher's own society. For twentieth-century Americans this was to mean an effort at harmonizing the common-sense view of the world with the latest scientific descriptions of nature. Had he known another sort of theology and philosophy, he might have concluded that the opposition between science and religion was, as he himself declared so many other dualisms to be, illusory and ill-founded or at least susceptible of a reconciliation on higher ground. As it was, he never looked again to "traditional" religion for an answer to what he once called the deepest problem of life: "The problem of restoring integration and cooperation between man's beliefs about the world in which he lives and his beliefs about the values and purposes that should direct his conduct."[13]

The main stages of his odyssey, described by himself as the passage from absolutism to experimentalism, have long been well known. Hegel was his first master; and although he eventually discarded idealism, he always retained the appreciation

---

[13] Dewey, *Quest for Certainty*, p. 255. The material of these paragraphs on Dewey's collegiate experiences is taken from his own account in Adams and Montague, *Contemporary American Philosophy*, Vol. 2, pp. 13, 19-20.

of process and the organismic logic which he learned more from Hegel than from Darwin. With these insights certain aspects of James's psychology fitted very neatly—the notion, for instance, that life, its development, and every organic function must be understood in terms of the organism's interplay with its environment. As Dewey would put it in his *Logic*, things live not *in* their environment but *by means of* their environment. Biological evolutionism meshed later with a parallel theory of social evolution, for from his friend, George H. Mead, Dewey learned a great deal about the importance of human relationships, of intercommunication and participation in common projects for the development of a "self" in man. Or, as both Dewey and Mead believed, not merely for the growth, but indeed for the very creation, of human personality.

All these matters had been part of the record for some time when, after Dewey's death, Max Eastman came forward with a striking story quite as illuminating and much more exotic than this account of the conventional scholastic influences. For two years after his graduation from Vermont, Dewey taught in a small high school in South Oil City, Pennsylvania. As Eastman tells the story:

> One evening while he sat reading he had what he called a "mystic experience." It was not very dramatic. There was no vision— just a supremely blissful feeling that his worries were over. When he tried to convey this emotional experience to me in words, it came out like this: "What are you worrying about, anyway? Everything that's here is here, and you can just lie back on it."
>
> "I've never had any doubts since then," he added, "nor any beliefs. To me faith means not worrying."[14]

---

[14] Max Eastman, "America's Philosopher," *Saturday Review* 36:24, January 17, 1953. In his youth Eastman was an assistant to Dewey while making graduate studies in philosophy and he speaks of Dewey as his "closest intellectual friend" during those four years *(ibid.)*. The incident which he relates has a curious parallel in the history of education. We are assured by such students

The incident is wonderfully revealing. Almost any interpretation of reality, of course, could maintain on its own terms that whatever is here, is here. The Christian, for instance, thinks of God as immanent as well as transcendent. Nevertheless in the context of Dewey's philosophy this awkward phrase seems intended as a nontechnical statement of the fundamental thesis of his naturalism, that the universe of being is no more than the totality of what is enclosed by the categories of time and space. This system is also an uncompromising materialism, although Dewey did not care for the term. "Why do I not come out frankly and use the word *materialism*," he once wrote, "since I hold that all the subject matter of experience is dependent upon physical conditions?" Only because the label implied metaphysical notions of substance, and of a dualism of spirit and matter which he considered so indefensible as to render the expression useless if not misleading.[15]

The depth and pertinacity of that youthful experience are also remarkable. The conviction engendered is said to have remained unshaken for more than seventy subsequent years, although on the evidence of Dewey's publications one would have judged that the transit from idealism to instrumentalism came later and took longer. It is certain, at least, that in the great

---

as Irving Babbitt that the key to Rousseau's thought is to be found in Jean Jacques' account of his celebrated experience in 1749 while he was walking from Paris to Vincennes. He had then the vision of his philosophic cornerstone, the intuition that man is naturally good and that it is by his institutions alone that he becomes wicked. The asocial accent in this is, of course, opposed to an essential Dewey position; but although some followers of Dewey do not like the suggestion, there are important similarities between these two altruistic and optimistic naturalisms and it is at least an odd coincidence that there should have been in the lives of both men crucial raptures with high significance for their thought. An earlier account of Dewey's experience, substantially the same as the version quoted here but with somewhat greater stress on the quasi-religious overtones of the incident, was given by Max Eastman in "John Dewey," *Atlantic Monthly* 168:673, December 1941.

15 Schilpp, *The Philosophy of John Dewey*, p. 604.

books of Dewey's maturity the problems which question the all-
sufficiency of this material cosmos and the moral autonomy of
social man are never even raised. They have been, as Dewey
liked to say, not so much solved as eliminated. The young man
musing over his books in South Oil City seemed to have made
his choice once for all and to have dismissed the perennial inquiries about the world and God, spirit and matter, time and
eternity. They were not susceptible of investigation by the techniques of biology, astronomy, physics, or chemistry; and since
no other method of valid inquiry was admitted, they were dis-
patched without review. This did not mean, of course, that they
were thereby subtracted from other men's consideration, and
Dewey was too levelheaded to suppose that it did. But for himself the matter was decided, and all ethical problems were
henceforth posed on a strictly secular plane.

If Dewey's universe is wholly material, it is not on that
account inert or fixed. Darwinism had convinced him, on the
contrary, that nature was radically evolutionary and although
uncertain, susceptible of at least some control for better results.
Indeed, this was the bequest Darwin had made to philosophy, for
by laying hands "upon the sacred ark of absolute permanency"
he had reinstated the ideas of change, genetic method, and the
mutability of forms. For Dewey the implications were revolutionary. In the first place, it swept out the metaphysical conceptions of being and knowledge which had reigned for two
thousand years. Or, as he put it even more spaciously when discussing the importance of scientific procedure for social betterment: "Intelligence after millions of years of errancy has found
itself as a method."[16] But above all, the application of Darwinism to philosophy issued for Dewey in a moral imperative. In
an evolving and perilous world men have to plan and struggle

---

[16] John Dewey, *Liberalism and Social Action*, p. 93. New York: G. P. Putnam's
Sons, 1935.

for possession of happiness. All sorts of obstacles are thrown up and must be circumvented. And since, as Christian moralists have often remarked, in practical matters no one solution exhausts every possibility, men are forced to pick and choose among alternatives. "Our constant and inalienable concern is with good and bad, prosperity and failure, and hence with choice."[17] Consequently human existence is profoundly ethical in character for the area of deliberate choice is precisely the area of morality.

Men had always realized, of course, that they lived in a world of hazards. Crops fail if there is too much or too little rain. Tigers prowl about the compound at nightfall. The raft capsizes in midstream. And for millennia before Darwin, people believed that by prudent option and skillful action they could partially direct their fortunes and diminish the uncertainties. But Dewey was convinced that the full range of this action was not appreciated until applied Darwinism postulated a cosmos, social as well as organic, in which everything is evolving and capable of issuing in success or failure. For on the one hand, life is seen to be everywhere in motion and pervaded by the need for an election; and on the other, there is a real possibility of selecting the most promising alternative, promoting its actualization, and learning from an observation of the consequences. Intelligent human activity implies just this capacity. In what Dewey himself called his behaviorism, mind is the sort of action stimulated by this endless encounter with knotty situations. So pleased, in fact, was Dewey with the value of the problematic as a spur to thought that he considered the depression of the 1930's, in spite of the tragedy that it brought into so many lives, a small

---

[17] John Dewey, *Experience and Nature*, p. 32 (Chicago: Open Court Publishing Company, 1925). See also Dewey, *Experimental Logic*, p. 73: "To place knowledge where it arises and operates in experience is to know that, as it arose because of the troubles of man, it is confirmed in reconstructing the conditions which occasioned those troubles."

price to pay if it would induce Americans to reflect upon the causes of the disorder, confusion, and insecurity which were, he thought, the outstanding traits of their social life.

It matters, probably, only to scholars if the readings of history which illustrated this analysis were excessively carefree. The major thinkers of the past would no doubt have been surprised to learn that they dwelt in a block universe where human freedom could hardly do more than pick its feeble way over a prison floor among the monolithic pillars of motionless forms and preordained outcomes. What counted for Dewey's development was his discovery in Darwinism rather than in the Aristotelian theory of act and potency, or the Hegelian dialectic, or the Christian view of history the crucial summons to an exercise of responsibility for the course of events. "To improve our education, to ameliorate our manners, to advance our politics, we must have recourse to specific conditions of generation," he wrote in a celebrated essay on *The Influence of Darwin on Philosophy*.[18] Many of the great metaphysicians would have agreed, of course, but they would not have granted that philosophy has no other function than the projection of hypotheses for social improvement. What he liked about Plato, Dewey noted, was the way even the highest speculative flights came back to earth with a social and practical turn. As the base for a preference this may be defensible enough, but there is less evidence that Plato himself valued metaphysics simply as a handy tool for trimming stones for the city of tomorrow.

For a philosopher, however, who thought as Dewey did and who could write, "Science . . . is the sole instrumentality of conscious, as distinct from accidental progress," American history during the past century must often have seemed a powerful confirmation of the pragmatic faith, if it did not, indeed, gen-

---

[18] John Dewey, *The Influence of Darwin on Philosophy*, p. 18. New York: Henry Holt and Company, 1910.

erate it.[19] From 1859 to 1952 John Dewey moved through several worlds. The Vermont of his boyhood was a community still self-reliant enough to engage growing children in a round of cooperative household and agricultural activities that provided, he said, the most rewarding part of his education until he entered college. As a young man he did graduate work in one of the oldest coastal cities. Later on he came to know the north-central region at a time when it was rapidly expanding, for he taught both at Ann Arbor and at Chicago about the turn of the century. Finally he moved on to New York, where he came up hard against the ambiguities in what he referred to as our "money culture."

Two generalizations have often been called upon to characterize this whole epoch. It was, in the first place, everywhere an age of astonishingly rapid growth, change, and technological success. Between 1860 and 1900 the population doubled, and before Dewey's death it had doubled again. At his birth a relatively small percentage of Americans were counted urbanites but at his death more than half were. During these decades the age of steam and steel began the transformation of the nation into an industrial powerhouse, and the succeeding ages of oil and the dynamo raised it to further heights of awesome size and strength. Railway lines and highways ran all over the landscape. The skyscrapers shot out of the rock and the corn out of the conquered prairies. The frontier was closed and the skyways were opened; the sound waves were exploited and the atom split. The American workingman perfected a pattern of organ-

---

19 Dewey, *Democracy and Education*, p. 266. See John Dewey, "The Supreme Intellectual Obligation," in John Dewey, *Education Today*, edited by Joseph Ratner, p. 287 (New York: G. P. Putnam's Sons, 1940): "Here is a most significant phase of the obligation incumbent upon the scientifically trained men and women of our age. When there is the same energy displayed in applying knowledge to large human problems as there is today in applying it to physical inventions and to industry and commerce, many of our present problems will be well on their way to solution."

ization and influence which punctured the larger part of the
Marxian prognostic. In culture and education the expansion was
just as compelling as in government and industry. By mid-
century America was not only a master of technology but the
home of distinguished writers, painters, and composers and the
seat of rich and productive universities.

At the same time, this was also a period in which the security of the individual seemed curiously diminished despite the
common prosperity. Freedom, too, was somewhat constricted as
men's fortunes were bound up with the increasingly complicated
problems of the great commonwealth. Development of technology and urban life meant an increase of interdependence. A
colonial farmer could boast that he produced himself all that
his family ate, drank, and wore. Today a single ice storm may
leave entire suburbs without heat, water, or power. The Great
Depression showed how intimately linked were the economic
fates of millions and how deeply they could all be shaken. After
the Second World War Americans found themselves ironically
exposed to fresh anxieties just because their country had become
so strong as to occupy, willy-nilly, front rank in the global fears
and strife. Doubtless the over-all balance sheet for the past century would show an unprecedentedly high level of physical comfort and security, even though war and depression might remain
like bloody question marks on the horizon. But like many other
observers, Dewey believed he noted a different sort of insecurity
growing, not merely in spite of or parallel to the industrial advance, but with some sort of positive correlation. The machine
age had suffocated the highly self-sufficient individual like the
eighteenth-century landholder—under a one-crop economy even
the farmer patronizes the chain store. At the same time, according to Dewey, science had unfrocked those old religious ideals
which formerly supplied people with a tranquilizing philosophy
of life, a sense of their place in the universe, and a safeguard
for satisfying social relationships in the family and the church

circle. "The loyalties which once held individuals, which gave them support, direction, and unity of action, have well nigh disappeared," he wrote. People were consequently bewildered and confused. It would be hard to find anywhere in history, he added, an age so "lacking in solid and desired objects of belief and approved ends of action as is the present."[20]

Had he lived to appraise the upsurge of interest in religion that marked the 1950's, Dewey might have qualified his factual descriptions, but he would have called the revival itself simply a failure of nerve and no real answer to the problem of individualism in industrial civilization. The real answer lay, he always thought, in a social reconstruction which would restore a tradition of freedom and equality of opportunity as defined in the secular terms of the eighteenth century. Growth of the machine had crowded out this spiritual factor, not because of any ineluctable necessity—it is childish animism to blame machines—but because in the actual historic event technology has so far been controlled by interest in private profits rather than by a concern to enrich the environment for all. The economic inequalities which result have poisoned the wellsprings of democracy and inhibited the proper exploitation of the industrial apparatus. If the situation could be radically healed, Dewey believed that new sources might be opened up which would more than compensate for those factors in our mechanized culture which seem now to involve some depreciation of the individual's inner security and depth.

Economic historians may find this analysis just as oversimplified and even erroneous as historians of philosophy find Dewey's exegesis in their field. But Dewey, at least, believed it and was consequently hostile toward the economic complex vaguely referred to as American industrial capitalism. Nothing

---

[20] John Dewey, *Individualism Old and New*, p. 52. New York: Minton, Balch and Company, 1930.

nettled him more than Bertrand Russell's bland assertion that instrumentalism is a philosophy tailored for Big Business. On the other hand, when he set himself to consider how a new individualism could be achieved and economic benefits more widely extended, he insisted that reform must begin with society itself. This of course is quite consistent with his stress on the creative function of the social matrix; but in elaborating it Dewey was rather unfair to those who would hold, as one statesman put it: "Only with self-mastery can we hope to master history." Dewey liked to pretend that such a view supposes that social abuses can be erased simply by regenerating individual consciences. Actually, of course, most reflective persons of whatever persuasion would agree that a simple outpouring of good will is no substitute for sound tax and minimum-wage laws.

In the interests of his polemic, however, Dewey often seemed to be insisting that society must *first* be made whole before men can be restored to integrity. He neglected the possibility of a reciprocal movement and consequently was open to the charge of circularity: until individuals are enlightened, society can't be improved; but until society is improved, individuals can't be enlightened. It remained for his friends to point out, as Sidney Hook does, that a sort of gradualism is possible. A few people see the light and help to bring about a bit of change. Then their tribe increases and more searching changes are possible. But this was what nearly everyone else had maintained, anyhow, although notions about the sources of illumination naturally varied. In any event, the twenty years between 1932 and Dewey's death in 1952 proved that a considerable amount of social change can be effected even without a majority commitment to a conscious instrumentalism. But Dewey himself was persuaded that the "imaginative formulation of itself" which best expressed American civilization was his own biological naturalism designed to serve as the ideological base of both personal integrity and social solidarity.

It is within the context of this conception of the American problem and this preferred avenue to its solution that Dewey's thought on the nature of intelligence and virtue and on the consequent role of the school is to be understood. Few philosophers have had as much confidence in and nourished such proud, high hopes for human intelligence as did Dewey. By an historical irony, it is true, he became widely misidentified with a spirit of soft pedagogy and the neglect of vigorous intellectual training; but he himself had actually put development of reflective thinking as the chief aim of formal education, just as his whole program for secular salvation was built on loyalty to intelligence as "the purposive reorganization, through action, of the material of experience."[21]

It is true, of course, that his concepts of intelligence and truth were different from those of the older epistemologies and those of common conviction. For there is a strong popular aversion to limiting knowledge to the referential alone. This will be apparent to anyone who has observed a pragmatist trying to persuade his audience that one knows a chair only by sitting in it or the past only as it is implicated in the present. But Dewey was not less an intellectualist just because his theory of intelligence was pragmatic. It was the same phenomenon in the real world to which he and his critics both pointed—that capacity for reason which, said Dewey, education must develop above all because the sum of its values makes the difference between a truly human life and that of a beast sunk in sensation and appetite.[22] For him, of course, this rationality is the distinctively human way of solving life's troubles by drawing up plans of action which one predicts, or hopes, will resolve the crisis. It is, he said, response to the doubtful as such. To be intelligent is simply to forecast the future. And if the plan of action does indeed

---

[21] Dewey, *Democracy and Education*, p. 377.
[22] John Dewey, *How We Think*, p. 78. Boston: D. C. Heath and Company, 1910,

dissolve the perplexity and effect a more satisfactory position in the moving stream of life, then it is true.[23]

The adjustment made by a sound use of the pragmatic method is secure and need not be made over again. Moreover, the knowledge gained in the confirmation of the hypothesis can be stored up for future use. It is, if you like, a truth possessed, funded meaning—but not irrevocable. It may have practical certainty, but logically speaking it always remains hypothetical. One speaks, therefore, of these idea tools as good or bad rather than as true or false, since what matters for their validity is whether or not they dissipated the difficulties. It must be remembered, too, that the purpose of any instrument is the work it effects. The aim of a knife is to cut. It is not the tool but the workman that has goals. Hence intelligence has no other end than intelligent activity itself, and education, which is basically a thinking experience, has no end either save the continued expansion of this instrumental power of thought.[24]

These perceptive analyses would doubtless have been less controverted had Dewey not proposed them in so exclusive a form. For after all, as Maritain has pointed out, Aristotle long ago distinguished two fundamental modes of intellectual operation: the practical and the speculative. The truth of the former does indeed lie in the success of the work. But when men are engaged in the reflective search for wisdom, they are convinced

---

[23] Dewey, *Quest for Certainty*, p. 224: "Many definitions of mind and thinking have been given. I know of but one that goes to the heart of the matter:—response to the doubtful as such. No inanimate thing reacts to things *as* problematic." Again Dewey writes in *Studies in Logical Theory*, p. 75 (Chicago: The University of Chicago Press, 1903) that the test of the validity of an idea "is its functional or instrumental use in effecting the transition from a relatively conflicting experience to a relatively integrated one."

[24] See Dewey, *Experience and Nature*, p. 154: "Truths already possessed may have practical or moral certainty, but logically they never lose a hypothetic quality"; Dewey, *Democracy and Education*, p. 192: "While we may speak, without error, of the method of thought, the important thing is that thinking is the method of an educative experience."

that there is possible a knowledge which consists in a vital, though not exhaustive, understanding of the nature of things as they are. Although Dewey grants that the practical exercise of intelligence may be satisfying in itself—as in the case of a re-search scientist—he rejects the notion of truth as a possession or disclosure of reality. He does not, of course, think of himself as a skeptic. For him the post-Cartesian problem of knowledge is "nonsense" because knowledge of extramental reality is sim-ply something we empirically *have,* as *Experience and Nature* declared. A man may be no more able to classify his cognitive experience than to diagnose his sickness as measles, but he can-not doubt that he is sick or that he has knowledge. Sometimes Dewey would grant the existence of a common and stable mini-mum of meaning—in the knowledge, for instance, "of the struc-ture of sticks and stones."[25] But for the most part the burden of his epistemology is faithfully operational. The real problem of knowledge, he thought, is a matter of learning what we need to know about the objects of experience in order to control them rather than to be controlled by them. Or, as he put it when epit-omizing the theme of his Gifford lectures, it is replacing the quest for certainty through cognitive means with the search for security through practical means.

What is most appealing in this theory, however, is not its rather arbitrary terminology nor its inflexible cadres but simply Dewey's forceful reminders of the relevance of knowledge for the business of life and of man's essentially active nature. Real-ist philosophers, to be sure, have always granted, not only the pragmatic function of thinking, but also the experiential mo-ment which necessarily initiates and supports that more spec-ulative moment which is really an extended reflection on the intelligible implications of experiential data. Still, it is true that the distinctive methods of practical intelligence were not much

---

[25] Dewey, *Philosophy and Civilization,* p. 5. See also Dewey, *How We Think,* p. 125.

explored by earlier philosophers although they were always appreciated by artists and scientists. Dewey not only devoted himself to a study of this operational employment of reason, but he
also accented its importance both for wisdom and for morals.
Many ethicians have taught that a neutral human act is impossible, since every authentic action involves knowledge and some
sort of choice and hence inevitably puts on a moral qualification. Dewey emphasized this position within his own system of
naturalistic morals. The world in process which he described
obliges men at every juncture to select the means leading to desired ends, for intelligence, he observed, is placed within the
procession of events. In such a world men are perpetually creative; it is themselves above all that they are fashioning.

These are healthy accents, for there is, perhaps, a tendency
to forget that reality is not wholly disclosed by contemplation
and that in any event the career of thought is indeed instrumental to the whole of human existence and loses its richness if
isolated from that context. Dewey pointed out that much of our
knowledge of this world is knowledge of the purpose and use
of things—a chair serves for repose, a wagon to cart objects
about. There is no particular reason why a man perceiving a
chair across the room should deny that this awareness is "knowledge," and useful as well. But it is also true that he knows more
about that chair when he sits in it. The example is trivial and
somewhat misleading, but there is another area in which the
principle is highly significant. For to borrow from Maritain
again, the pragmatic insight into the processive nature of our
experience and the way it conditions our effort at understanding
really finds its most apt application in the moral order. For
there is a realm in which knowledge not completed by action is
seriously truncated, thin, and unreal. "I should rather have com-
punction than know how to define it," said the author of the
Imitation. But unless he lived it, he could not be said to have it,
and unless he had it he could scarcely be said to know it.

It is not surprising, then, that problems of human conduct were so central for Dewey. Whenever he talks of knowledge the thought of its ethical implications is not far from his mind. He once observed, for example, that the chief task of a teacher is to see to it that the greatest possible number of ideas acquired by young people are so acquired as to become true motive forces of conduct.[26] But to say as much is to raise at once the ancient questions about the definition of the good man and the norm of morality. Dewey's effort, of course, was to develop an autonomous, naturalistic morality and to show how moral categories themselves evolve as tools for adjusting the conditions of human life. As intelligence develops, he thought, men cease plunging blindly after desired objects and learn to look ahead and to reduce their conflicts with one another by fashioning concepts of right and obligation, duty and law, good and bad. If you ask, then, how these results are appraised and whence they derive their authority, Dewey would first remind you that men are essentially social. To live at all they must live in society, not as coins in a box but as plants live in sunlight and soil. But it is this community life itself which demands those relations of cooperation and subordination which the moral concepts express.

The over-all good is measured by the degree to which social life makes possible the individual growth of the members of society. It may be objected that some people relieve their tensions and appropriate their personal good at the expense of others. Dewey would reply, however, that these socially undesirable actions are not real goods and no true solution for the individual's problem. For since a man can exist only in and through society, he must follow the line demanded by social interests, for he cannot have the better life save insofar as the

---

[26] John Dewey, *Moral Principles in Education*, p. 2 (Boston: Houghton Mifflin Company, 1909). See also Dewey, *Democracy and Education*, p. 418: "The most important problem of moral education in the school concerns the relationship of knowledge and conduct."

society in which he lives is bettered and he himself becomes a better social being. The strongest reinforcement of duty's demands, said Dewey, is the realization of the interests of others that are bound up with it. It is not, he wrote in an early work, the mere individual as such who establishes the final end or provides standards of goodness. It is rather the complexion and process of the social life he shares with others which settles these things. Or as he put it on the next-to-last page of his best-known book, a man has to be good for something; he can't just be "good." And the something for which he must be good is fruitful participation in society, so that what he gets from living with others balances with what he contributes.

Nevertheless a certain confusion remains as long as the concept of constructive social action cannot be evaluated by some independent and secure measure. We are not reassured when we are told that men are born "with a natural desire to give out, to do, and that means to serve," so that, if their education and community life engages them properly, the ideal moral character will inevitably flower.[27] In our time we have seen too often the aberrations into which the good citizens of totalitarian states can fall through loyalty to the frenzied mystique of their civil society. Dewey, of course, was critical of all totalitarianisms because they hobbled the associative possibilities of men. Yet there remains some sting in the well-known criticisms which Russell and Santayana made of his ethics. For one does find in Dewey a tendency to value the individual almost wholly in terms of his social competence and to exalt the powers of the community until it becomes its own final sanction. The result is that the

---

[27] John Dewey, *Ethical Principles Underlying Education*, p. 16 (Chicago: Reprinted from the Third Yearbook of the National Herbart Society by the University of Chicago Press, 1903). It was this remark which Irving Babbitt seized upon in proof of a resemblance in Dewey to the spirit of Rousseau's optimism. See Irving Babbitt, *Democracy and Leadership*, p. 313, n. 1 (Boston: Houghton Mifflin Company, 1924).

majoritarian rule not only acknowledges the just and the good but constitutes them.

Conscious, perhaps, of these uncertainties, some of Dewey's acute followers grant that there are certain immediately valid goods which support standards—friendship, wisdom, beauty, courage—but these must never be considered as ultimately and unconditionally good. This may only mean that any good action needs to be judged in the light of all its circumstances, as most people would admit. It is more to the point to ask why these values can be called immediately valid in the first place. Dewey himself seemed to ground the entire moral structure on a master value, postulated rather than demonstrated or delineated in detail: a society in which the greatest possible number of people would have the greatest possible opportunity to develop, in and through their social experiences, the wisdom and prudence which bring wide-ranging, lasting satisfaction.

It is only logical that this philosophy which makes of ideas plans for action and which interprets conduct in terms of tension solving for the sake of richer, subsequent experience should have a pronounced futuristic strain. It is, in fact, a good case of what D. W. Brogan has called the permanent American passion for dealing in futures. This is not an entirely happy quality; for the present, which is all we ever have, is pretty well gutted if it is no more than a depot on the journey to tomorrow. Dewey liked to insist, therefore, that knowledge of an object's instrumental properties is not "inherently adverse" to an appreciation of goods and goals. His philosophy of art, too, tried to exploit the intrinsic joys of the creative activity itself and at least succeeds in proving that not even Dewey could explain the aesthetic experience in purely instrumental terms.

The Christian will find this moral theory least alien in its emphasis on social responsibility. For this is, after all, a secularized version of the precept of fraternal love and represents a sound reaction against excessive individualism in morals and piety. But Dewey's belief that the whole intellectual and moral life could be faithfully modeled on the single pattern of the scientific method will win no such general acceptance. He himself often seems to suppose that everyone will react to a moral dilemma much as an elderly Vermonter would. He does not appear to realize how many of his own ideals of honesty, service, and devotion had come to him through the Christian tradition and were neither the results of an instrumental search nor common elements of every civilization. *Human Nature and Conduct,* for instance, discusses the case of a man trying to make up his mind about gambling. The negative hypothesis is preferred on the ground that the results would be socially undesirable. But this solution might have little force for a confirmed fan-tan player in another culture where it is taken for granted that husbands may define their rectitude in egocentric fashion and are not expected to defer to the feelings of their wives. On the other hand, if intelligence cannot to some extent grasp those aspects of reality which are not susceptible of physical manipulation, then much that matters dearly to many men is beyond reach. Whole zones of thought and of existence are forever unattainable if the only mode of inquiry is that of forecast, test, and filing of results. The prospect would then be somber indeed for those who do not share Dewey's faith that men need no more than the full range of associative experience for integration and salvation.

WORK AND EDUCATION

The most decisive influence on his own intellectual history, Dewey once said, was his interest in the practice and theory of education. This interest centered on the elementary school for the sensible reason that the quality of the foundation determines the soundness of the whole structure. It so fused all his other concerns that for many years, by Dewey's own testimony, the fullest expression of his philosophy was an educational treatise, *Democracy and Education.* That book aimed at formulating and applying to educational problems the theory its author believed to be implied by a democratic society. It has already been re-marked that for him this critical sifting of the values and beliefs of a culture was precisely the philosophical task. If done badly it would be no more than a purblind rationalization of preferred institutions and local prejudices, but it could be done critically. The bond between education and philosophy is, then, an organic one. For education is transmission of a culture, and since phi-losophy evaluates that culture—is, so to speak, its critical uni-versalization—it is at least possible that philosophers might decide what ought to be transmitted and thereby exercise some control over the course and quality of the future.

Since Dewey's life and thought were dominated by devotion to ethical ideals and to the exercise of intelligence for the reali-zation of these ideals, he is in fundamental agreement with all great educational theorists, all of whom cherish these generic goals. The intellectual aim of education, Dewey maintained, "is entirely and only the logical in this sense; namely, the forma-tion of careful, alert, and thorough habits of thinking." From the moral standpoint, "the ideal aim of education is creation of power of self-control."[28] Novelty appeared, of course, when these propositions were spelled out and one learned that "there is no such thing as genuine knowledge and fruitful understand-ing except as the offspring of *doing*," or that morality is organ-ized capacity of social functioning.[29] These specific differences, however, do not cancel Dewey's basic kinship with other phi-

---

[28] The comment on the intellectual aim of education is found in Dewey's *How We Think*, pp. 57-58 and is, indeed, the theme of this whole book. The formula-tion of the ethical aim is from Dewey's *Experience and Education*, p. 75 (New York: The Macmillan Company, 1938).

[29] See Dewey, *Democracy and Education*, pp. 321, 181 and Dewey, *Ethical Prin-ciples Underlying Education*, p. 8: "The individual is always a social indi-vidual. He has no existence by himself. He lives in, for, and by society, just as society has no existence excepting in and through the individuals who con-stitute it."

losophers of education equally devoted to the twin vision of wisdom and goodness.

Guided by these goals, Dewey was not opposed in theory to a schooling which accented book learning. In *Democracy and Education* he grants that there is much to be said for concentrating the actual classroom hours upon books if during the rest of the time children are involved in valuable occupations calling for a cooperative sharing of labor and responsibility. For then the total educational experience, always as wide as life itself, would ensure development of habits of instrumental thinking and social skills. Dewey observed that in his own boyhood children found many educational opportunities in the life of the family and in the township. Nowadays the humanistic influence exerted by a multitude of household and community tasks has largely disappeared. Consequently another sort of society must be developed, the school society, which will serve as the essential social medium for shaping character. "Apart from participation in social life, the school has no moral end or aim."[30] On the elementary level this will best be done by introducing children to operational thinking, the key to social reconstruction, and to experiences in cooperation. And in both cases a preeminently sound method will be that of manual work. Why?

It does not seem possible to analyze work without keeping the product as well as the process in view. Dewey, however, true to his preference for process and instruments, diminishes, though he does not deny, the role of the product and insists that work must not mean such subordination of activity to result as will rob the former of all significance. With education in mind, he sets up a genus: active occupation. Its species include work, play, and art. Or perhaps this active occupation should be thought of as a continuum whose moments, though separate, are not to be sundered. At least Dewey thought the gap between

---

[30] Dewey, *Moral Principles in Education*, p. 11.

manual activities and those presumed to be more intellectual, as they are certainly less strenuous, was the illogical outcome of historical accident. In his *Logic* he argues that the civilizations of Assyria, Babylonia, and Egypt created false dualisms between the empirical and rational, theory and practice, common sense and science, by this distinction of the "higher" techniques of priests and savants from the "lower" work of carpenters and pottery makers. The Greeks were a mixed bag. Their distinction between philosophical contemplation and an inferior practical shrewdness was regrettable, but they are also to be credited with the discovery of scientific method and instrumental arts of control based on the study of nature and pointed toward social applications. A failure of nerve followed the period from Homer to Aristotle, and a collapse into two millennia of obscurantist supernaturalism, until the modern world emerged from the gloom in the sixteenth century.

It was Dewey's conviction that the artificiality of these distinctions between work and loftier intellectual employment is evident when one realizes that the only fruitful method of thought, the method of the physical sciences, is essentially the method of manual work itself. For scientific knowledge, Dewey argues in *Experience and Nature*, is knowledge of "nature in its instrumental characters" and it was in work that men first grasped this operational—that is to say, intellectual—phase of things. The man who labors uses objects as tools and thus he perceives their authentic meaning, which is instrumental. When this insight was sophisticated by science, it changed the world; and were it transferred to realms of conduct, it could work wonders as great as those which have transformed jungles, swamps, and deserts into cities, parks, and flowering gardens. In fact, by ignoring a Genesis text which shows that Adam had been obliged to work even before his disobedience, Dewey can amuse himself with a little joke. For, he says, it was only after our forebears had sinned and been forced to toil in order to provide for them-

selves that men really became godlike, knowing good and evil.
For only then were they compelled to record nature's behavior
and start their evolutionary ascent by learning to use tools and
read signs.[31]

Of all active occupations, work is the most valuable because
it is the most universal. Since almost everyone has to work,
everyone gets some initiation into pragmatic thinking and some
opportunity for social maturation. At least this is possible.
Dewey wisely observed that, if most men have found their job
only a necessary evil to be endured, the fault is not in work itself but in the conditions surrounding it. His own concern was
for the psychological rather than the economic aspects of labor.
The economic perspective puts too much stress on the product.
It is true, of course, that work is precisely that active occupation
which includes a conscious regard for results. But when these
consequences are unrelated to the activity itself, work turns into
constrained effort and the assembly-line robot is preoccupied
with his wages, not his manufacture. Ideally, it is the work
product itself, the natural goal of the process, which should
govern the whole activity. Dewey's analysis here is not unlike
those of the Marxist and the Thomist. Play, he writes, is free,
plastic. But in work the definite, external outcome desired must
be held to persistently. "If a child is making a toy boat, he must
hold on to a single end and direct a considerable number of acts
by that one idea." The product itself incarnates this master idea.
But that insight is beyond the pieceworker, for it is grasped only
when one has followed the process through from raw material
to completed artifact and thereby gained "the intelligence embodied in finished material."[32]

Since work, art, and play are not to be sharply differen-
tiated, Dewey's fundamental recipe for the ambiguities vitiating

---

[31] Dewey, *Experience and Nature*, p. 121.
[32] Dewey, *Democracy and Education*, pp. 238, 234.

actual work experience calls for an infusion of the latter with the characteristic attitudes of play and art. Work, indeed, came first and devised operational methods. But when play borrowed this methodology, it did not have to concentrate on the goal with such businesslike intensity. It discovered the joy in the activity itself and could return this insight to labor. Art is nothing more than work permeated with the play attitude, so that not only the product but also the process is inherently enjoyable. For occupations can be congenial if this pattern of beginning, sequence, and climax is understood. Men hunted in the beginning for their livelihood, but afterwards for sport. On this analysis, the aesthetic quality ought to pervade any sort of work even though its results are undistinguished. Dewey was too hardheaded not to see that this is a nearly hopeless ideal under current conditions of machine production. But he was also convinced that the humanizing power latent in an understanding of applied science would counteract the bad effects of mechanized labor if men could once grasp the whole process of which their work was a part.

It is clear, then, that Dewey would not subscribe to Marx's notion of engaging school children in formal industry for the sake of economic gain. Dewey was interested in the educational virtualities of work activity freed from the constraints of the profit motive. He approved, certainly, of household chores, but he did not equally approve of the work opportunities provided by modern cities, for these, he said, were actually apt to be anti-educational. In *The School and Society* he makes the point with a slightly different terminology. There he distinguishes *work*, which focuses on the external result, from *occupation*, which focuses on the related mental and moral states and the growth involved in reaching that result. The work activities in the school program, then, are occupations in this latter sense and are prescribed for the development of children, not for their emolument nor for the convenience of future employers. Elementary education should provide everyone with this experience of technics, which is not at all the same thing as a trade training. It does not aim to transform girls into milliners or cooks and boys into mechanics or carpenters. Rather, said Dewey, the school should "utilize active and manual pursuits as the means of developing constructive, inventive and creative power of mind."[33] The medieval schoolmen distinguished the development of the worker from the development of the material, the *perfectio operantis* from the *perfectio operis*. Dewey, perhaps, would have suspected that this distinction too much divided the continuum of subject and object. Yet he himself is not far from such a distinction when he recommends manual arts, not for the enhancement of wood and fabric, but for the humanization of student craftsmen.

When the children in the laboratory school kept a garden or followed the production of textiles from raw cotton to the stitching of shirts, they were neither training for a job nor contributing to the necessary sustenance of life, although both these purposes might have been indirectly furthered. They were reproducing some form of work carried on in the social order, but they were doing so for the sake of its inherent civilizing potential. Dewey believed that young children are most easily and naturally introduced to the rules of sound thinking through the concrete logic of action. Such a device is ideal because it maintains a just balance between the analytic and practical phases of experience and fixes the child's attention on the relationship of means to ends, that instrumental passport to knowledge. All we ever know, Dewey believed, is a subject matter determined in the context of a specific problem, and therefore it is useless to address oneself to global and illusory questions about the nature

---

[33] John Dewey, "Learning To Earn: The Place of a Vocational Education in a Comprehensive Scheme of Public Education." *School and Society* 5:334, March 24, 1917.

of being or the meaning of the universe.[34] Intelligence is developed only by grappling with the problems of real life, and these call for application of that technique which is employed by both science and manual work.

So long as children do not have this humanistic experience outside the school, they must have it within. There the work projects may be deliberately archaic, for the intellectual value of handicrafts is superior to that of machine tooling. Children must follow these projects from start to finish if they are to understand fully the function of instrumental skills, since any "whole" is simply the functional development of a situation. They must be allowed to set their own goals and devise their own means, for only thus is judgment matured. Their very mistakes will help to acquaint them with the limit of their abilities. In a word, the educational significance for intelligence of active occupations lies in the fact that they represent things to do, not studies, just as their significance for character education lies in the fact that they typify social situations, not precepts.

For these work activities in the school contribute both to the understanding of moral values and the actual nurture of ethical fiber. Since the method of work is the method of science and this, in turn, the method of authentic knowledge and conscious progress, it ought also become the method of individual and social morality. Those who understand the procedure used in work, understand the technique for resolving their own consciences and for constructing the environment which effectively nourishes good men. So far as the practical aspects of moral education go, work projects are uniquely significant because they are embryonic recapitulations of social life. They serve,

---

[34] John Dewey, "Some Implications of Anti-Intellectualism," *Journal of Philosophy, Psychology and Scientific Methods* 7:479, September 1, 1910. Here Dewey remarks that instrumentalism "involves the doctrine that the origin, structure, and purpose of knowing are such as to render nugatory any wholesale inquiries into the nature of Being."

therefore, as an introduction to that cooperative activity which is the most powerful educator of character, even as it is the principle of human community. If you observe children at play, wrote Dewey, you will see that they are generally engaged in reproducing some social occupation—pretending to keep house or a store; building or baking or exploring. This universal childhood interest is the natural foundation on which to build for ideal character. Not, as Marx would have it, because work is itself the basic and ultimate human activity, but rather because in and through work something more precious and more fundamentally human finds expression: the desire to live in cooperative friendship with others. Work, for all its importance, is not the noblest value. Men must work indeed if they are to live, but there is more to life than this. It is rather the function of work, Dewey wrote, first to sustain life and then to supply it with some margin and thereby "to provide a permanent home in which all the higher and more spiritual interests may center."[35]

---

[35] John Dewey, *The School and Society*, revised edition, p. 136. Chicago: The University of Chicago Press, 1915.

CHAPTER IV

Work the Servant
of Leisure

On the eve of his eighty-fifth birthday in October 1944 John Dewey was interviewed by a respectful reporter from the *New York Times*. The conversation, as detailed next day, was pleasantly civilized. Dewey, indeed, had confessed himself somewhat pessimistic about the prospects for permanent peace, but he was characteristically confident that democracy would survive and that a better world lay ahead. At one point, however, a certain chill made itself felt. What did he think, Dewey had been asked, about the attacks made on his educational philosophy by Dr. Hutchins of the University of Chicago? "President Hutchins," was the grave reply, "calls for liberal education for a small elite group and vocational education for the masses. I cannot think of any idea more completely reactionary and more fatal to the whole democratic culture."[1]

For anyone who has followed, even casually, the history of educational theory in twentieth-century America this incident neatly symbolizes one of its perennial themes, that ancient but lively struggle between two divergent outlooks popularly, though inaccurately, labeled traditionalism and progressivism. For

---

[1] *New York Times*, October 20, 1944. Dewey's summary of Hutchins' position was actually not an entirely fair one.

95

Dewey's influence, great as it was, did not go uncontested during the past sixty years. There were always writers at hand to insist that if education, especially in the colleges, hopes to rescue men from the ambiguities and perils of modern society, it must put the individual person in first place and see more in him than his social dimension. It is impossible, they warned, to elevate human behavior by manipulating cultural conditions unless the prime effort is directed at changing people interiorly. It is unrealistic to think that one can transform society without transforming men and women through the medium of traditional liberal education. Sentiments of this sort came frequently from college presidents and deans, from religious educators and advocates of adult education, from the philosophers in the older tradition of American idealism as well as from literary humanists like Irving Babbitt and neo-Aristotelians like Robert Maynard Hutchins.

The debate has been concerned not so much with the broadest aims of education as with their interpretation and the methods of achieving them. After all, in that birthday interview Dewey had remarked that progressive education "stands for the most solid, enduring discipline that comes from growth and power in self-discipline," and to this all his critics would have answered amen. But canyons are cut when it comes to defining these terms and spelling out concrete programs. Earlier that same year, in May 1944, Dewey had sent a somewhat longer indictment of Hutchins to a Conference on the Scientific Spirit and Democratic Faith. This message began with a firm reiteration of his own methodological monism: the potentialities of the scientific method will not be realized until it is made the supreme agency for direction of collective human behavior. In parallel fashion, the potentialities of vocational education will not be realized until it is suffused with a liberal spirit and filled with a liberal content through an emphasis on its scientific and "universal social-moral applications." But this whole crucial

development is threatened, said Dewey, by the reactionary feu-
dalism of President Hutchins so clearly bent on restoring those
miserable dualisms of thought and action, the intellectual and
the practical, the liberal and the servile arts.[2]

Actually, as Dewey must have known, the movement championed by Hutchins was not so much a reaction as a particularly
spectacular flare-up of an ideology never decisively eclipsed
even though at the elementary- and secondary-school levels it
had suffered some loss of prestige. Yet its newer formulations
were not simply echoes of Aristotle and Quintilian, Erasmus
and Vives, Newman and Matthew Arnold. For the twentieth-
century defenders of the classical liberal arts could not entirely
ignore those problems of work and technology which contemporary civilization raises so imperiously. But though they had to
acknowledge the presence of such questions, they would not
agree that either work in particular or pragmatic action in general constitutes man's most distinctive perfection. For them work
is indeed a means, and one whose value lies precisely in its
power to purchase freedom from itself. Correlatively, it is the
main task of general education to equip people for the creative
employment of that fecund leisure time. For the good life, as
Adler said, *"depends on labor,* but it *consists of leisure."*[3]

During the past half-century these themes have been vigor-
ously expounded by Irving Babbitt from one quarter and by the
partnership of Hutchins and Adler from another. It is significant, though, that these writers have tried to link educational

---

[2] *New York Times*, May 28, 1944.

[3] Mortimer J. Adler, "Labor, Leisure, and Liberal Education," *Journal of General Education* 6:45, October 1951. For a similar remark see Robert M. Hutchins, *The Great Conversation: The Substance of a Liberal Education*, p. 14, in Robert M. Hutchins, editor, *Great Books of the Western World* (Chicago: Encyclopaedia Britannica, 1952): "Work is for the sake of leisure." In a re- nowned library's copy some indignant hand has neatly penciled in beside this sentence the comment: "Monstrous!" It is like Mr. Hutchins to arouse strong feeling in his readers.

theory, somehow or other, to a theory of labor and its role in life. May this have been because they were Americans rather than citizens of Periclean Athens or Renaissance Florence? Their solutions, it is true, were rather extrinsic. They did not illuminate or medicate work from within, but tried either to widen the notion itself or to clarify its reciprocal relationship to leisure and liberal studies. Babbitt, for instance, maintained that true leisure is not a matter of relaxation or reverie but vigorous engagement in the highest sort of "work," moral work, the strenuous ethical effort at self-control which is far superior to mere utilitarian labor. Hutchins and Adler, for their part, want leisure to be employed in deepening the life of learning begun in the liberal-arts college. But this pursuit of liberal learning will have beneficent resonances in the zone of work. At the very least it will serve, said Adler, to cure a man's discontent with the work he does and his need to kill time. And perhaps there is a more vital connection than this one of simple compensation, for Hutchins has argued that the civilization of intelligence through philosophy and letters will enable men to humanize their work by understanding it reflectively.[4]

There are, of course, profound differences between Babbitt's humanism and that of Hutchins and Adler, and not even the most determined concordism can level these off. The critical movements they captained kept up a steady bombardment of contemporary naturalism—but not from the same trenches. Babbitt only wanted to enlarge and complete naturalism by restoring certain specifically human elements which the "pure" naturalists were trying to eliminate. Metaphysics and theology were no friends of his. Man, he said explicitly, must be made the measure of all things. Hutchins and Adler, however, decisively rejected the basic naturalistic postulates and affirmed,

---

[4] See Adler, "Labor, Leisure, and Liberal Education," p. 45 and Hutchins, *The Great Conversation*, p. 16.

indeed, that man cannot hope to practice even the natural virtues consistently without divine aid.[5] The time-honored dispute over the primacy between intellect and will also divides these two systems sharply. Babbitt defended human reason against undue depreciation by those whom he skewered with epithets as primitives, humanitarians, Rousseauians. But he insisted that the intellect itself was subordinated to a certain power of "vital control," a higher will presiding over man's lower impulses and governing a distinct imaginative power which alone intuits true norms for life. Hutchins and Adler, however, are persuaded that intelligent reflection upon the real world reaches certain permanently valid disclosures about nature, man, and human conduct. In the thirties, indeed, their faith in reason was boundless. As a young man Hutchins complained that our common bewilderment is a result of our not having tried reason at all, whereas salvation is to be had in a return to intelligence. More recently, it is true, he has spoken less sanguinely about the possibilities of such a return, although he would judge it still the best natural hope. In a postwar broadcast over the BBC he remarked:

> Life is a chaos, a jungle. The mind of man revolts against bewilderment and finds ways through the jungle in the form of clear ideas and positive convictions. These become the effective guide of existence.[6]

---

[5] See Robert M. Hutchins, *The Atom Bomb and Education*, pp. 13-14 (London: National Peace Council, 1947) especially: "I doubt if any single man, to say nothing of the whole world, can practise Aristotle's Ethics without the support and the inspiration of religious faith. . . . Because men are animal, because the flesh is weak and life is hard, the virtues cannot be consistently practised without divine aid." See also Mortimer J. Adler, "In Defense of the Philosophy of Education," in *Philosophies of Education*, The Forty-first Yearbook of the National Society for the Study of Education, Part 1, p. 221 (Bloomington: Public School Publishing Company, 1942) and Robert M. Hutchins, "The Philosophy of Education," in Robert N. Montgomery, editor, *The William Rainey Harper Memorial Conference*, p. 35 (Chicago: The University of Chicago Press, 1938).

[6] Hutchins, *The Atom Bomb and Education*, p. 13.

Both these schools professed an admiration for science but deplored what Babbitt called a one-sided intoxication with it. They observed that modern man looks out on whole stretches of his life not devoted simply to the earning of a living. The really critical task, therefore, of contemporary education, especially at the collegiate level, is to prepare men for the best use of their ample leisure. To this end Babbitt suggested a program heavily weighted with studies in world literature, while Hutchins and Adler advocated a basic curriculum equally attentive to the social and natural sciences and to metaphysics. They propose, besides, that this intellectual diet be made available for all citizens through a vast adult-education program built about the Great Books. If men and women, Hutchins has argued, are to fulfill their political responsibilities intelligently, they require a rational understanding of the true and the good. He reaffirms his argument by saying that universal suffrage makes every man a ruler, but "if every man is a ruler, every man needs the education that rulers ought to have."[7]

Of course, this Aristotelian doctrine which makes work the servant of leisure and leisure the active cultivation of intellectual excellence is familiar enough and may seem very vulnerable if one assumes, as Veblen did in his brilliant and corrosive critique, that liberal education is equivalent to a conspicuous and nonproductive consumption of time. But it is just such an equivalence which Babbitt, Hutchins, and Adler in their several fashions would reject. Their urgency has little in common with a Petrarch or with Veblen's own ironic detachment. As much as Marx and Dewey, their interest in education is an expression of their larger concern for our human condition in an anxious age. This lends more than ordinary vigor to their recasting of traditional themes as a somewhat closer inspection may make clear.

---

[7] Robert M. Hutchins, *The Conflict in Education*, p. 65. New York: Harper and Brothers, 1953.

IRVING BABBITT AND THE SEARCH FOR STANDARDS

> Traditionally the Christian has associated his liberty and his faith in a higher will with grace . . . I myself have been trying to come at this necessary truth, not in terms of grace, but in terms of work, and that on the humanistic rather than on the religious level.[8]

When Irving Babbitt died in 1932 his reputation was secure among those sympathetic to his thought, but the thought itself had had its hour and was passing into a diminuendo. Still, Babbitt cannot be written off too quickly, for in the 1950's the New Conservatism (like him, better at demolition than construction) has revived his name and some of his ideas. Dominant among these ideas was the undarwinian conviction that the goals of life deserve more attention than its origins. First in importance, Babbitt liked to say, citing Aristotle, is not the seed but the guiding ideal of the perfect flower. He might reasonably have supposed that his own career confirmed this view, for in pursuit of his aims he progressed from a rather uncertain background into the role of a commanding academic figure, the tenacious defender of unswerving principles, the humanistic apostle of "poised and proportionate living." During the first ten years after his birth in Dayton in 1865, Babbitt's family moved frequently as his father experimented with various kinds of employment. There are some indications that the father's philosophy influenced the son by way of reaction. The older man was gregarious and his political sympathies were socialist in character. But all his life Babbitt distrusted and sharply criticized this sort of humanitarianism. He believed that the welfare of society depended less upon unselective sympathies than upon men's recognizing the need to govern themselves by determined standards. When a friend once contrasted this view with those of his optimistic father, Babbitt retorted: "You can't size up

---

[8] Babbitt, *Democracy and Leadership*, p. 316.

these eupeptic lovers of mankind in this offhand fashion—you should see my father working his way through the crowd to get a seat in the Elevated."[9]

When Babbitt was eleven his mother died and for the next five years or so he lived with his maternal grandparents on an Ohio farm. When his father remarried, Irving joined him in Cincinnati and finished high school there. In 1885 he enrolled at Harvard and his life after graduation was spent entirely in the academic world. He taught for two years in the College of Montana, an educational outpost with about a hundred students. A year of oriental studies in Paris was followed by another at Harvard during which his friendship with Paul Elmer More began. The school terms of 1893-1894 found him teaching romance languages at Williams and the next year he returned to Harvard to progress up the ladder to a professorship of French. The ascent, however, was not without commotion, for Babbitt considerably riled some of his colleagues by the polemics which sauced his exposition of unpopular ideas.

On the other hand, the picture which Babbitt's friends drew of him was consistent and attractive: a big, handsome, blond man rather bent in a scholarly slouch, courtly in manner, dogged and endlessly brilliant in argument; a teacher of enormous power and influence. He was also one of those writers who put a great deal of personal flavor into their books and one cannot read Babbitt without feeling his force. In his writing he is often witty and almost always striking, although his enormous erudition is not everywhere exact. His argumentation is direct and wonderfully spiced with what Norman Foerster called his instinct for ruinous quotation. It is also extremely repetitious,

---

[9] William F. Giese, in Frederick Manchester and Odell Shepard, editors, *Irving Babbitt: Man and Teacher*, p. 24 (New York: G. P. Putnam's Sons, 1941). The various memoirs in this collection of personal reminiscences of Babbitt are not titled but only numbered. This one is the first.

as Babbitt's comrade in arms, More, acknowledged. The author of these books had made up his mind early and changed it very little, so that the themes set forth in his first volume appear even to his last and sometimes they are all squeezed into a single short essay. The reader often imagines that he has seen these sentences before and at times he literally has, for the same choice paragraph will find a place in several essays and the same apt quotation will decorate several contexts.

The inspiration of all this intellectual effort was the desire to outline an ethical humanism which could support morality without recourse to religion. The core of such a humanism was to be certain perennial standards achieved by an intuition of the permanent aspects of reality which lie beneath the shifting manifold engaging the senses. For this intuition Babbitt needed to turn up some faculty of the real as an escape hatch from the confinements of dusty essences and mere appearances. So it happened that he was drawn into philosophizing although he did not consider himself a philosopher. In his teaching of French literature (which More said he studied chiefly to annihilate) Babbitt had concentrated on the play of ideas and their historical interconnections. This led him into comparative literature and thence into an inquiry after common norms applicable in different contexts. That investigation conducted him, in turn, into the wider field of general philosophy, for it involved, he said, one's attitude not merely toward literature but life.

But though he, a literary critic, had been caught up by these larger problems because the times were parlous and the professional philosophers bankrupt, Babbitt was suspicious of all branches of philosophy save ethics and all methods not largely practical. Life mocks at the metaphysician, he announced; but the problem of conduct may yet be approached experimentally. Actually, he had a rudimentary metaphysic of his own to offer, one of will and action in defense of the proposition that "the good life is not primarily something to be *known* but something to be *willed.*"[10] Its purpose was twofold: to avoid all those extremes that had toppled so many philosophical towers and to come, said Babbitt, at a humanism which should be both positive and critical. Positive, because it would work strictly from experience and accept the autonomy of man; critical, because all conclusions were to be tested pragmatically in terms of their relevancy for the goal of happiness.

For the central problem of life, as Babbitt saw it, is the problem of how the individual is to be happy—happy now, not in some distant and problematic future. There had been, he thought, three general approaches to this question. The traditional religions, according to Babbitt's highly colored and exaggerated readings, have proposed total renunciation of all sense appetites for the sake of interior peace. This is much too stiff for the humanist. At the opposite pole is pure naturalism either of the Baconian utilitarian sort which finds happiness in the exercise of power and the gospel of service or the sentimental Rousseauian brand which would let loose the flood of impulses. Both are blind alleys. Babbitt believed that one could recover the necessary balance and spiritual discipline by adopting a third attitude, the humanistic posture taken by an Aristotle or a Confucius, which is a mean between complete abnegation and complete abandon, between pure traditionalism and mere modernism. "Life in the humanistic sense means to live moderately, sensibly, and to the best advantage in the society of other men."[11] But this is possible only if a man exercises enough restraint to avoid ruinous extremes. Since restraint supposes

---

[10] Irving Babbitt, *On Being Creative: And Other Essays,* p. xxxvi (Boston: Houghton Mifflin Company, 1932). See also Irving Babbitt, *Rousseau and Romanticism,* pp. xiv-xvi (Boston: Houghton Mifflin Company, 1919). Babbitt argues here that the epistemological problem cannot be solved abstractly and metaphysically but can be solved practically in terms of actual conduct.

[11] Irving Babbitt, "Experience and Dogma." *Saturday Review of Literature* 7:287. November 1, 1936.

norms for the guidance of self-discipline, the philosophical inquiry of critical humanism becomes a search for a set of modern
standards—that is, a search for the element of oneness beneath
the glittering surface of the flowing many.

In its heyday, when the new humanism championed by Babbitt was attracting considerable attention, it seemed to some a
nasty throwback to medievalism, to others fascistic, and to still
others an unexpected ally of Christianity. Yet it is clear enough
that Babbitt was fundamentally closer to Dewey, for instance,
than to orthodox Christianity. Both men had behind them as a
kind of personal experience the nineteenth-century destruction
of the old religious certainties of Protestantism, and with earnest
intensity they both sought to build a new secular temple for the
orphaned spirit. They accepted the view that religion had been
interred, decently or not, and that the chief business at hand was
to lay more acceptable foundations for right conduct. So it was
that Babbitt, despite his disagreement with Dewey on many
points, could write: "All those who are striving to achieve
a modern outlook on life should be able to concur in his
[Dewey's] programme up to a certain point."[12] And of his own
work he had written in his first book: "In general the humanist
will not repudiate either sentimental or scientific naturalism; for
this would be to attempt an impossible reaction. His aim is not
to deny his age, but to complete it."[13]

Babbitt agreed with Dewey that the critical examination of
experience is the only admissible authority, but his concept of
this experience was quite different from Dewey's and he hoped
for more from the examination. He insisted that "experience"
must include not only the data of the physicist but the introspec-
tive intuitions of the humanist, as well as the funded wisdom of

---

[12] *Ibid.*
[13] Irving Babbitt, *Literature and the American College*, pp. 258-59. Boston: Houghton Mifflin Company, 1908.

the human race preserved in its literatures. This experience, moreover, must be approached with a variety of techniques. One must be rational in opposition to those who overstress the unconscious, the spontaneous, and the instinctive. But one must also be intuitive in opposition to the frozen metaphysics of classical tradition, for only by intuition can one reach the truths beyond reason's grasp. One must be modern, but not a modernist—able, therefore, to seize "the abiding element through all the change in which it is implicated," for it really "exists even though it cannot be exhausted by dogmas and creeds, is not subject to rules and refuses to be locked up in formulae."[14]

Babbitt hated all extremes and was endlessly fertile in pointing up the way in which top-heavy positions destroy themselves. He could always see the defects in "pure" anything—pure naturalism, pure democracy, or pure classicism. Once he cited Luther's comparison of mankind to a drunken peasant on horseback who, if propped up on one side, slumps over on the other. As Babbitt saw it, this is pretty much what is always happening in the history of thought, and in his own writings he is continually running from one side to the other trying to balance the good points in polar positions. This constant concern to "avoid the indolence of extremes" makes him a tonic for readers, but it must be admitted that his destructive analyses are much more impressive than his original remedies.

In keeping with his wide-ranging interests Babbitt found something to approve of in Christianity even though he rejected its claim to be a revealed religion. He liked, for example, its insistence on a teleological element in human existence and its appreciation of certain dualisms which he stressed himself: between man and nature and between the higher and lower impulses in each individual. His chief complaint against people like Dewey was that they had badly analyzed experience; did

---

[14] Babbitt, *Rousseau and Romanticism*, p. 391.

not really understand the nature of knowledge, action, and morality; had failed to grasp the symbolic truth in religion; and by their cultivation of the mirage of "service" had fallen into the sticky well of sentimental illusion.

Nevertheless, despite the talk about experience, the autonomy of man, and the avowals of positivism, Babbitt's philosophy strikes the reader as excessively bookish. The experience he consults most often is that which is "transmitted to us in consecrated masterpieces," and his characteristic themes are generally sounded in a literary context. He talks of Emerson when proposing the discontinuity of man and the infrahuman world; of Buddha when emphasizing ethical activity for self-conquest; of Confucius and Aristotle when advocating restraint; of Burke and Washington when deploring totalitarian democracy; and of Rousseau practically all the time but particularly when hammering on the "doctors of relativity." It is true that such a key doctrine as the dualism of flesh and spirit is proposed as a psychological fact but hardly demonstrated to be such. It is certainly possible to argue cogently for the existence in man of two sorts of tendency or appetite, one following upon sensation (Babbitt's "will of the flesh") and the other following upon intellectual knowledge (the "will of the spirit"). But Babbitt does not thoroughly canvass those facts of common experience which would support this distinction so central to his own system. He prefers to test this and other controverted doctrines by a pragmatic criterion based on a vague sort of historical experience. Can pure naturalism make men happier than ethical humanism with its doctrine of the higher will? Let us see by examining the actual consequences of living according to the Buddha and according to Rousseau, for "the supreme maxim of the ethical positivist is: By their fruits shall ye know them."[15] The only

---

[15] *Ibid.,* p. xvi; and see pp. 237-38 for the notion that the record of the past should be a school of judgment for us.

trouble is that the evidence is dreadfully sketchy and of a sort that only bibliophiles can assess.

Still, this literary thicket ought not be allowed to obscure Babbitt's distinctive ethical motivation, which is so relevant for questions of culture and education. He is grappling, after all, with basic problems of life and happiness and the literary criticism is only the envelope for the real message, a warning to his contemporaries that they were in danger of losing their freedom and debasing their humanity. For a culture without stable standards, he declared, turns democracy into egalitarianism and prepares the propitious moment for the imperialistic leader, while the individual who fails to live by the law of measure not only destroys himself but weakens the fabric of the whole community. What Babbitt is really proposing is not so much a save-the-liberal-arts-college as a save-man-and-the-world program. He may not have suggested his humanism as a substitute for religion, but he certainly offered it as a practical alternative for people like himself who found no existing religion appealing. The content of this offering will appear if one studies Babbitt's ideal man, the well-tempered ethical humanist.

He is, to begin with, a man who emphasizes the will and its work of self-discipline. Your humanist, said Babbitt, thinks more highly of his power to act upon himself than he does of his power to act upon the world. It has already been noted that this doctrine of the pre-eminence of a will quality is the pivot of Babbitt's sketchy psychology and, in fact, Dom Grosselin has shown that it is the heart of his thought.[16] We do not get from

---

[16] Oliver Grosselin, *The Intuitive Voluntarism of Irving Babbitt: An Anti-Supernaturalistic, Anti-Intellectualistic Philosophy, passim* (Latrobe: St. Vincent Archabbey, 1951). See, for one of Babbitt's characteristic comments, this from the introduction to *On Being Creative*, p. xxviii: "If one admit a higher will at all, one must grant at the same time that the rôle of reason in its relation to this will is not primary but at most instrumental, that reason cannot hope to formulate finally what is by definition above it."

Babbitt any systematic explanation of the two wills nor of the higher and lower imaginations said to be correlated with them, but the general idea is clear enough. Introspection discovers to the humanist both a drive toward simple, undifferentiated expansion and indulgence and another tendency which makes itself felt, in relation to the first, as a will to refrain and is therefore called variously the higher will, vital control, the inner check, the ethical will, or the ethical self.

The good humanist recognizes that in any wise scheme of life this higher will must rule. And that for a single reason: it is the way to be happy. It does not require the mortifications of the saints but only such limitations on desire as have been found to make, in two ways, for real happiness. For this practice of restraint contributes to that inner poise and balance which spares a man all the dreary excesses and black abysses of the romantic primitive. At the same time, it develops that texture which we have in common with one another and suppresses our bizarre differences. This makes it possible for the humanist to commune at least with other humanists, and thereby solves the problem of human loneliness.

The universe in which the humanist dwells blends an ever-changing oneness which is reality with a diversity which is illusion, and it is his business to penetrate to those elements of stability on which standards are grounded. But Babbitt explicitly associates this intuition with the influence of the higher will, which is for him the power really linking men to the center of things. Consequently the true humanist is not so much contemplative as a man of action, a strenuous man albeit the strenuousness is of an ethical and interior sort. The result of all this effort is to make him at once a comprehensive yet selective harmonization of intellectual culture and moral distinction. The "inner check" has subdued in him the madder flights of pure temperament without quenching the latter entirely. The humanist indulges all the human interests—but selectively. He is equally disdainful of the sweaty enthusiasms of the do-gooder and the blindness of defenders of majority options. If you suspect him of being something of a snob, you must remember that Babbitt denounced French neoclassicism for combining Aristotle and the dancing master and for repressing natural impulses which needed only control. If you suspect him of being merely a fastidious hedonist, you must remember that Babbitt's own ideal was St. Francis de Sales, who had fulfilled, he thought, Pascal's recipe for human excellence by harmonizing in himself opposite virtues and occupying all the space between. Still, Babbitt also liked Castiglione's remark that the make-up of the gentleman should combine an element of aloofness and disdain, *sprezzatura*, a characteristic not commonly considered Salesian.

The humanist has, however, an inner gyroscope which centers him on his course, and this is humility or "inner obeisance of the spirit to something higher than itself."[17] In *The Masters of Modern French Criticism* Babbitt observes that for St. Paul, Christ was the living intuition of a law set above the ordinary self but that the humanist defers to a model within, a set of standards derived by discriminating between what is worthwhile in one's nature and what is merely eccentric. He remains silent, however, about the exact lineaments of this exemplar—the specific content of his code. All we are told is that some people can study the ideal philosophically but that for most the easiest way to come upon it is through good literature.

Although the humanist is an individualist in the sense of making his personal happiness the primary reference, he is not indifferent to the wider common good. Indeed, he feels that he wonderfully upholds it. His efforts at self-control are based, to be sure, on his obligations not to society but to himself.[18] No

---

[17] Irving Babbitt, *The New Laokoon: An Essay on the Confusion of the Arts*, p. 211 (Boston: Houghton Mifflin Company, 1910). Discussions in praise of humility are in Babbitt's *Democracy and Leadership*, pp. 158-85, 186-90, 298-99.

[18] Irving Babbitt, "Sociology and Humanism." *Nation* 102:620, June 8, 1916.

other social foundation is possible, said Babbitt, than this one of self-interest, for Dewey's faith in native altruism is sheerest delusion. Without reviving the doctrine of original sin, the humanist will recognize that psychological division in man which finds expression in sharp conflict between selfish and generous impulses. This is Diderot's "civil war in the cave." To dismiss it by transforming the struggle of the individual with himself into a struggle of the individual with society, thus making the environment responsible for moral failure, is a fatal mistake. The social value of humanism is said to lie precisely in its radical cure of that egoism which ignores the standards of good conduct. Educators, therefore, must remember that they benefit society only by developing the power of self-control in its individual members. If they want, for instance, to restrain our gifted but rapacious entrepreneurs, it is pointless to try to turn them into philanthropists after they have made their fortunes at the expense of the commonweal. The real hope, wrote Babbitt in *Literature and the American College,* lies in inducing the future Harrimans and Rockefellers to "liberalize their own souls, in other words, to get themselves rightly educated."

The social values of the humanistic program can be spelled out in a bit more detail. For one thing, the good humanist would share, according to Babbitt, in the spirit of scientific progress and social pity which has swelled up in the last two centuries, but he would not make absolutes of these. More significantly, humanistic education itself provides the ground for a true community among men and at the same time it nurtures the good leader so necessary in a democracy. Genuine ethical communion, national or international, requires development of the inner life, for only when men subordinate their personal exaggerations to the essential common to them all do they overcome the anarchic individualism which otherwise drives them apart. The cultural and ethical agreement of humanists is itself a social stabilizer. The obvious difficulty is that this union is bound to be restricted. The majority in Greece or elsewhere, Babbitt once observed, is almost sure to be one-sided and therefore unsound. This is quite a different outlook than that, for example, of Christianity, which understands itself to be, not simply an ascetical code for gnostics, but a religious society whose membership is potentially as wide as humanity itself and whose way of life invites all men to high holiness. Moreover, the Buddhism which Babbitt so admired is described by scholars as a scheme of conduct for the average man who will find in his daily routine plenty of chance to subordinate the lower nature to the higher. Babbitt cannot easily extend his program this way, since it supposes a long immersion in literary studies and the multitude is never likely to be in a mood to dive into such pursuits.

Humanists might retort that at least they can produce eminent individuals for leadership. Leaders are going to appear anyhow and the final test for a democracy, as Tocqueville knew, will be its ability to encourage the superior. Babbitt was persuaded that his ethical humanism would turn out men prepared to serve the common good rather than personal gain or factional advantage; men who emphasize the inner life and are ready to render their fellow citizens the best of all services—good example. In fairness to him it must be remarked that this defense of an elite is not a defense of hereditary aristocracy, privilege, or class society. He wanted, it is true, to mobilize the sages, but he intended to scrutinize carefully the quality of the recruits. Democracy has no place, he said, for snobbish distinctions of family or rank. But it should be—and the liberal-arts college reflecting its spirit should be—a fair field with no favors in which men of quality naturally gravitate to positions of leadership. One does not need to be a sentimental naturalist, however, to chafe at Babbitt's tone when he observes that it is proper and inevitable for the man who works with his mind to rule the man who works with his hands, and that laborers benefiting from invention and industrial organization ought to shun the agitators who would stir up envy. Doubtless, those who work with the mind are ruling the world, and even the labor unions have seen a generation of leaders grow up without much firsthand experience of manual labor. Still, Babbitt's comments betray a bit too much *sprezzatura* and are too innocent of qualification. His whole theory of humanism, however, and its value for personal development, its social utility, and its historical antecedents is summarized in the doctrine of work suggested here. The actual problem of the relation of education to the labor which supports life is, of course, practically volatilized in this treatment, but it will be instructive to see why this is so.

The good humanist, on his own reckoning, is a self-reliant fellow very busy measuring up to the standards he has intuited and tested. Consequently his inner life is most intense, since both his spiritual and material success hinge on this ethical exertion. When Babbitt reflected on the character of this moral effort, he concluded that it was, in fact, a form of work consisting in "the superimposition of the ethical will upon the natural self and its expansive desires."[19] Did it occur to him also that this notion would happily adapt a Renaissance ideal to the American temperament by enrolling humanists in the labor force at the loftiest level? Of course, it would also require some adjustment of the common concept of work, and so Babbitt argues in *Democracy and Leadership* for a Socratic dichotomization dividing work into two categories, "inner" and "outer," which are like moments along the same scale.

"Outer work" is expended upon material nature and governed by the law of things. It is utilitarian and a source of property. For the most part it engages physical effort and is often susceptible of a quantitative description. Since this sort of work is much discussed by Bacon, Locke, Rousseau, and their friends,

---

[19] Babbitt, *Democracy and Leadership*, p. 197. Babbitt's fullest treatment of ethical work is found in pp. 188-213 of this book.

we are not surprised that Babbitt pays it scant attention. His chief concern is with work in the spiritual sense, "inner work," the effort at self-control in obedience to the human law. To identify work with manual labor is a fallacious reduction of the concept to its lowest terms, says Babbitt. Actually, the ethical exercise of restraint for the sake of humanistic *pleroma* is superior to all other forms of work. Babbitt never makes clear under what genus this inner employment and economic labor are both to be subsumed, possibly because he nearly shoulders the common notion out of the picture. Perhaps the analogous note is this: in utilitarian work man imposes his will upon the material world and in ethical work upon the stuff of his own life. In one case he produces things; in the other, himself.

The ideal and the primacy of ethical strenuousness had been historically asserted, said Babbitt, by Confucius, Buddha, and Aristotle as well as by Christianity. But he believed that Christianity had subverted the ideal of a strictly human form of moral enterprise by its doctrine on the necessity of grace for meritorious action. In pursuing the classical terms of Christian theology Babbitt was not at his happiest. He obliterates such distinctions as that between naturally good acts and those elevated by grace to effectiveness for salvation, and he ignores the necessity of human cooperation with this grace. Still, Christianity had at least recognized the nobility of this work of the spirit, and it would be the business of humanists to recover that truth on some positivistic basis.

If they do so they will have strengthened the fiber of the whole democratic community, for democracy flourishes only when men are free and only those skilled in the practice of humanistic moderation are authentically free. Society should, therefore, encourage men engaged in this ethical work and even relieve highly endowed individuals of the necessity of manual labor so that they might give all their time to this higher occupation. "It is in fact the quality of a man's work that should determine his place in the hierarchy that every civilized society requires. In short, from the positive point of view, work is the only justification of aristocracy."[20] The standard of the American frontier has here been appropriated by the ethical humanist, who gives it a new meaning by turning it nearly inside out.

In the light of his philosophy Babbitt might easily have concluded that the most important part of any education is training for ethical work. He did not care for Plato's identification of knowledge and virtue, although he admitted that ignorance is a root of much evil. Moreover, he believed with Plato that the corrosive influence of environment and crowd psychology could only be withstood by a systematic counteroffensive. To this end Plato had proposed a state-controlled school system; and although Babbitt distrusted the totalitarian strain in this scheme, he was strongly devoted to the ideal of education. Making his own the expression of a colleague, he said that education was the one altruistic activity the humanist embraced. For the humanist, as he elsewhere remarked, "is not fighting for the past; he is fighting for a civilized present and a civilized future."[21] But if the men of the future are to like and dislike the right things, they must be educated in the appropriate habits almost from infancy.

Babbitt's thought on education never received its final form, for death prevented him from returning to this, the subject of his first book. That book spoke only of the liberal-arts college which Babbitt knew at first hand, and its themes are sufficiently familiar now. The college was thought of as a middle ground between the preparatory school and university specialization. As such it was to be a place of general education, for one must be a man, said Babbitt, before being an entomologist. The college would be small, selective, and democratic, but a democracy

---

[20] *Ibid.*, p. 202.
[21] Babbitt, "Sociology and Humanism," p. 620.

honoring talent and achievement. Its curriculum would most
certainly not be elective. Eliot's famous remark about a well-
instructed youth of eighteen being better able to choose his own
course than anyone else had a horrid fascination for Babbitt. It
seemed to him quite mad. The curriculum he himself proposed
would represent a humane selection of studies reflecting, as *Literature and the American College* put it, "in some measure the
total experience of the race as to the things that have been found
to be permanently important to its essential nature." This meant
for Babbitt, in 1908, the study of literature with emphasis on
Latin and Greek classics approached rationally rather than in
the fashion of neoclassicism and the German grammarians.
Reading and memory would be much cultivated, and Babbitt
confidently maintained that it was an open question whether any
direct training in English style could be so effective as translat-
ing Latin. Above all, the college should provide opportunity for
that true leisure which is equally opposed to indolence and util-
itarianism. The climate of leisure is simply the climate of effective thought for the sake of effective self-discipline. It is the
country of the spirit in which a man broods over his own experience and that of the race in order to discover the path to the
future and to happiness.

The details of this program are certainly quite conventional
and hardly equal to the amplitude of Babbitt's general aims.
Perhaps he would have expounded his educational theory and
even set it within another dimension had he lived to write that
final book, but even in his earliest pages there is some appreciation of the educational problems peculiar to a modern, industrialized democracy. In such a society the common needs of the
populace have to be met while at the same time gifted persons
are offered the sort of training that will develop their best potential. One might put it crudely by saying that education for
intelligent "followership" is as necessary as education for leadership. For his part, Babbitt was not simply a reactionary oppo-

nent of the machine age, for he saw the gift of leisure it could underwrite, and no gift was dearer to one who relished Aristotle's conviction that a man cannot practice virtue if he is living the life of a mechanic or laborer. But Babbitt was not persuaded that the dehumanizing forces of mechanized industry could be compensated for by socializing the economy or that the human cog could be adequately uplifted and consoled by a scientific education illuminating the whole assembly-line process. For such a man would still be fragmented at his work and his education would not have made him less a hopeless wanderer in the wide world. The real solution, Babbitt believed, must lie in opening up to more people the opportunities for ethical growth in true leisure. Beyond this broad comment he did not go; but in recent decades Robert M. Hutchins and Mortimer Adler have worked out somewhat more completely a solution which is quite similar to his.

THE RADICALISM OF HUTCHINS AND ADLER

Wherever you touch education, said Robert Maynard Hutchins a few years ago, it fades into something else. Its aims, for instance, will mirror the aims of the society in which it is conducted and its philosophy is built from relevant blocks of general philosophy—metaphysical, moral, and political. Consequently both he and Mortimer Adler, his comrade in so many intellectual wars, have always insisted that the troubles of the schools are only the inevitable reflections of troubles in our civilization; and they have underscored the obvious but easily neglected fact that the most critical questions for any educational theory are those which concern the nature of man, his community life, and his pursuit of significance and joy. What has distinguished them from many other critics of contemporary culture and education is the practical energy and the barbed eloquence which they have brought to bear on problems in both the academic and civic order. They have torn a humanistic theory out of the scholarly enclosure and set it down with a loud bang in the market place, although in the process of acquiring volume and clarity the theory lost something in depth and nuance. This was understandable enough, of course, in the case of men whose concern for the schools is only part of a larger concern for the common welfare.

A celebrated sentence from the first page of Hutchins' best-known book, *The Higher Learning in America*, observed that the most striking fact about that learning was the confusion besetting it. All his more recent writings have reaffirmed this verdict: educational theory and practice continue to be chaotic. But if the schools are running a fever, we should suspect some virulent disorder in the social organism. Hutchins, indeed, discovers and denounces various social aberrations; and even his critics find the indictments forceful. We have, he has often said, education for all but widespread ignorance, unparalleled industrial productivity but continued and even greater poverty—taking the world as a whole. At the levels of communication and transportation the world is made one but in more essential matters bitter disputes divide men and nations. There is a great outpouring of scholarship and writing but philosophies remain mired in conflict, and instead of class divisions we have new ones induced by those rival forms of specialization which make it so difficult for the engineer to understand the poet.

All these evils are due in great measure, Hutchins believes, to our society's weakness in its intellectual foundations. "The most characteristic feature of the modern world," he wrote a quarter of a century ago, "is bewilderment. It has become the fashion to be bewildered. Anybody who says he knows anything or understands anything is at once suspected of affectation or falsehood."[22] In the intervening years Hutchins has not with-

---

[22] Robert Maynard Hutchins, "The Issue in the Higher Learning." *International Journal of Ethics* 44:175, January 1934.

drawn his earlier diagnosis of the crisis in terms precisely of a failure in rationality. It is clear, however, that he has significantly qualified it. The Hutchins of 1956 certainly sounded rather different from the Hutchins of 1936 when he wrote: "Since we are agreed that it is more important to be good than to be intellectual, and that it is hard, if not impossible, to be good without being religious, and since we want higher education to exert a moral and religious influence through its pervading tone, it would seem to follow that men should not be appointed to the faculties of colleges and universities unless they are moral and religious men."[23]

Still, he has not abandoned that earlier campaign in defense of reason, a campaign which he once prosecuted so enthusiastically as to give the impression that he believed that to be intellectual simply *is* to be good. This effect was due partly to Hutchins' penchant for colorful, unilateral emphases and partly to his professional interest in college education. For while the tradition which he espoused grants the need for ethical and religious formation, it nevertheless makes the cultivation of intelligence the schools' chief business.

But twentieth-century schools, it appears, are having a great deal of trouble keeping their minds and energies focused on this precise intellectual task. The strains and anxieties interwoven with American life have created corresponding hazards for education and for several decades now Mr. Hutchins has been surveying the results with tireless acerbity. A spirit of materialism, we are told, showing itself in an excessive love of money and a simple-minded belief in progress, has combined with the pressures of industrial civilization to push collegiate education into an overemphasis on vocationalism with an exaggerated esteem of science. It is forgotten, he remarks in *The University of Utopia,*

---

[23] Robert M. Hutchins, "Religion and Higher Education." *Commonweal* 64:322, June 29, 1956.

that thought and art are the highest activities of the human race. Instead, specialization has been allowed to crowd out general liberal education, with a consequent weakening of the intellectual base of our community. Philosophical diversity prompts educational theorists to adopt a philosophy of "no philosophy at all" while the demands for social and political conformity encourage adoption of a quite inadequate educational objective: adjustment to the environment. Such a goal has little value in itself and is useless in a rapidly changing society. To make the aim the satisfaction of immediate needs is no better and is doomed to futility anyhow, since there are far too many evanescent "needs" and far too much information for the schools ever to meet or supply.

From 1929 to 1951, the years when Hutchins was first president and then chancellor of the University of Chicago, he and Adler preached a rather radical remedy for the nation's political and educative ills and even accomplished a certain amount of change. Their purpose, often expounded, was the reinstatement of human reason, as they understood it. This reinstatement was to be accomplished for young people by a specific kind of liberal collegiate education and for the mature by an adult-education program fired by the same purpose of directly cultivating intelligence. If reason were thus restored to eminence, there would be some hope, they thought, of arriving at a sound philosophy of life and education. Even more important, this restoration would be the key to creation of an intelligent electorate and therefore the key to a solution of our social dilemmas. It is doubtless true, said Hutchins, that schools generally do no more than preserve the accepted values in a given community, but this does not mean that such preservation is an ideal, for the values may be illusory. An informed citizenry, however, can lift itself by its bootstraps, for if "a country decides to move into a different spiritual world, it can use the educational system to help it get there," and the schools, in turn, are capable of

raising the level of society by improving the individuals who
make it up.[24]

The primary political ideal, for instance, ought to be determination of the common good in the light of reason. In a democracy, however, this presupposes a reasonable people and
imposes upon the educational system, as its first duty, the nurture of rationality.[25] The education of these democratic rulers,
as Hutchins worked it out, would include, at the college level,
grammar, rhetoric, and logic (reading, writing, and thinking, as
someone has said), along with philosophy and the social and
physical sciences. The lower schools would prepare for this
college; the professional and technical institutes cap it.

In its purest form this recipe, however traditional it may
once have been, was certainly not characteristic of American
collegiate training in the second quarter of the twentieth century. How much influence the Chicago offensive had on its behalf is still debated. Hutchins' friends believe he brought back
the idea of some general education before specialization. His
critics scoff and reply that the basic notion had never been lost.
In the field of adult education a distinctive impact is perhaps
easier to discern. An acute Italian journalist, Luigi Barzini, Jr.,
decided that Americans were ending not only their space but
their time isolation because he had been struck by the interest
in historic thinkers which inspired the study groups working on
the Great Books. In 1952 there were, according to a popular account, some two thousand such groups, and their program has
been closely associated with the names of Hutchins and Adler,
who, if they did not invent it, at least sold it.

This interest in adult education was natural enough, since
many of Hutchins' and Adler's own distinctive positions were

---

24 Robert M. Hutchins, *The University of Utopia*, p. 100. Chicago: The University
   of Chicago Press, 1953.
25 Robert Maynard Hutchins, *Education for Freedom*, p. 59. Baton Rouge: Louisi-
   ana State University Press, 1943.

arrived at by arduous self-education after the years of formal schooling had past. In a sketch called *The Autobiography of an Uneducated Man* Hutchins has clearly suggested that his personal scholastic history helped generate his convictions about the deficiencies of American higher education. For although he had grown up in an academic milieu (his father was an Oberlin professor) to an academic career meteoric in style, his own education began in earnest, he said, when at the age of thirty-two he started to read and teach some of the Great Books in various schools of Chicago University. A few years earlier, while teaching at the Yale Law School, he had puzzled over the philosophical foundations of legal axioms and these inquiries led to his first meeting with Mortimer Adler, some years his junior. According to journalistic accounts Adler had been caught up in an energetic intellectual career ever since grade school and was already absorbed in various great books when he went to Columbia. There, and in the following years, Adler's path crossed not only Dewey's but those of two ancestors of the Great Books idea. At Columbia he was first a student and then an instructor in the two-year general honors course which John Erskine had initiated after the First World War. Later, Adler conducted a similar course for an adult group meeting in a church basement and he also lectured at the People's Institute when it was under the direction of Everett Dean Martin. Martin (1880-1941) was a former minister who dedicated himself to the task of imparting some traditional humanistic culture to everyone. His ideals were not unlike those of Babbitt, who has been described as an advocate of the Christian way of life with Christianity left out.

The Chicago program contained echoes of these earlier experiments but it had characteristics of its own. One of its centerpieces, for instance, was the conviction that the core of liberal education ought to be a planned and progressive diet of reading in those books which have shaped and partially embodied the tradition of western civilization. When the college student or the adult in a study group takes up one of these books, however, he is not presumed to be looking for relaxation or aesthetic delight. Considering the inclusion of Aristotle, Galen, Harvey, and Marx, to cite but a few names, he is not likely to find either. It is rather the discipline of intellectual effort provided by a course of stiff reading that is wanted, and wanted as the training which fits a generation to cope with the problems of a frantic hour. The proponents of the curriculum believed that the power of sound thought and expression is acquired only by practice and that the ideal practice is had when students center their reading, writing, observation, and discussion around the issues raised by great thinkers. The books are, said Adler, borrowing an image from Stringfellow Barr, for the young student what a bone is for a puppy and he concluded emphatically that "unless the bone is a real one, a bone that can challenge the puppy to get his teeth in, there will be little agitation and even less sharpening of teeth."[26]

Yet there is more to it than this notion of pure mental exercise. That of itself would not have so exasperated experimentalists. The added controversial element is suggested when Adler writes: "The books are to be read because they are as contemporary today as when they were written, and that because *the problems they deal with and the ideas they present are not subject to the law of perpetual and interminable progress.*"[27] No other single assertion of the Chicago partners so inflamed naturalistic critics as the assumption that there are perennial truths which can become the common possession of all inquiring minds. But whether they are to be looked upon as intellectual gym-

---

[26] Mortimer J. Adler, "The Order of Learning," in *The Philosophy of Christian Education,* Proceedings of the Western Division of the American Catholic Philosophical Association, Fourth Regional Convention, San Francisco, 1941, p. 114. San Francisco: The Association, 1941.

[27] Mortimer J. Adler, "The Crisis in Contemporary Education." *Social Frontier* 5:144, February 1939.

nasiums or as repositories of basic ideas or as the best prelude to professional specialization, the Great Books were to occupy an honored position in Hutchins' model college. This college, he said, should be devoted to single-minded pursuit of the intellectual virtues by that two thirds of our young people who can profitably learn from books. It would accept them after two years of high school and enroll them in one of three faculties of emphasis: metaphysics, social science, or natural science. Every student, however, would be required to take some work in each of these three areas while accenting the one most relevant to his own vocational intentions. The whole program would be unified by metaphysics, since the modern secularized university cannot be integrated through theology as the medieval school once was. The metaphysics itself, alarmed naturalists noted, was that of the Platonic-Aristotelian-Thomistic tradition and therefore, presumably, implacably hostile to science and progress. Adler insisted, in rebuttal, that the Hutchins' program agreed with progressivism in allowing place for novelty and advance because it required the heritage of the past to be ever corrected and augmented. In recent years, too, Hutchins has frequently been careful to defend the inclusion in the university of not only "debate" (reading and discussion) but also "discovery" (research and invention).

Some of these ideals were actualized at Chicago during Hutchins' administration, and both he and Adler were godfathers, in a way, to the experiment in a Great Books curriculum at St. John's College, Annapolis. But in one of those melancholy footnotes that history writes we learn that after Hutchins departed to the Ford Foundation and Adler to the task of summarizing all western thought in a *Summa dialectica*, many of the distinctive features they had sponsored were suppressed. No longer, for instance, may a bright tenth-grader move straight into the University of Chicago. These reversals, the press reported, caused some commotion and parades of collegians carrying banners emblazoned with an old Hutchins' challenge: "Too few have the courage of my convictions."[28]

In the 1930's, however, when these convictions were still young and yeasty, he himself gave them hearty voice. Those were the days of the incendiary manifestoes which so enraged the opposition. "The task of education is to make rational animals more perfectly rational," Hutchins would say. And given his own definition of the terms, Dewey might have assented. But he would have warmly disagreed with further sentiments of this sort: "The substance of liberal education appears to consist in the recognition of basic problems, in knowledge of distinctions and interrelations in subject matter, and in the comprehension of ideas."[29] The implication here that ideas are rather independent of concrete, problematic contexts, that they are aseptic objects of study like mathematical formulae, led Dewey to charge Hutchins with defending the total aloofness of a university from the affairs of life. Actually, Hutchins was never disposed to isolate either himself or his school from social problems, but it is also true that he was partly responsible for the bad, not to say violent, press that he often received. For he is endowed with a stinging rhetorical talent and a flair for making his points in a manner more shattering than measured. Very likely busy administrators have not much time for prolonged reflections, but in any event Hutchins' expositions often lacked depth and balance for all their glittering brilliance. Thomists, for instance, shuddered at his highly unqualified and ambiguous formulations precisely because these were popularly accepted as accurate expressions of their own tradition.

Yet Hutchins' strength has also lain in these sweeping assertions, that dogmatic tone and frosty mockery, those extreme and

---

[28] *Time* 61:49, May 18, 1953.

[29] Hutchins, *The Great Conversation*, p. 3. For the remark immediately preceding see Hutchins, *Education for Freedom*, p. 37. This is a common theme in the writings of Hutchins and Adler.

horrible examples which recur so regularly in his pages: "The educational program for school janitors at Teachers College, Columbia, or for majorettes at the University of Oklahoma, or for beauticians at Pasadena City College, or for circus performers at Florida State University, or for teachers of driving in the University of California." He wanted to emphasize a point and he wanted to be heard. It is rather doubtful that he could have been any other way, for, as Milton Mayer pointed out, President Hadley of Yale had said much the same sort of thing earlier and no one listened because he said it politely. In another place and at another time Hutchins' criticisms and emphases might have been different. But looking around him in the thirties, he felt that, while Whitehead was right in principle when he said that the university must mate itself with action, American universities had greatly overdone it. "They are mated to so many different kinds of action," Hutchins wrote in the *Atlantic Monthly* in the fall of 1936, "that nothing but a few divorces can save them from the consequences of their ardor."

Chicago itself is particularly significant in this story because the university to which Hutchins came, associated as it was with the characteristic work of Dewey, Mead, Veblen, and Watson, seemed a major sanctuary dedicated to the dogma that true knowledge is scientific knowledge. Although Hutchins and Adler firmly professed esteem for science and gave it ample space in their curricular proposals, it would still be possible to sum up their distinctive work by saying that they raised the question of whether or not science itself is sufficient either theoretically or practically.

They raised it, of course, with considerable asperity, so that, while the Chicago papers sometimes berated Hutchins for communist sympathies (as regional chairman of the first National Labor Board in 1933 he had found in favor of a striking bus drivers' union), John Dewey gravely deplored his fascistic mentality, and at that, Dewey was more restrained than many commentators. When they first came to Chicago, Adler wrote, he and Hutchins found an academic center in which there was indeed a great unity of outlook but very little diversity, and when they tried to introduce some of the latter the result was conflict without community. These rather bitter experiences perhaps confirmed their view that education should somewhere along the line, preferably in the college, introduce everyone to a common tradition of learning, so there would be certain areas in which each man could understand his neighbors.

Philosophies constructed in time of war are apt to be fiercely one-sided, and Hutchins and Adler plotted theirs under vigorous academic shellfire. Perhaps this explains why it leaves even sympathetic readers uneasy. Their broad aims, like most broad aims, are unexceptional enough but not particularly enlightening. One can agree that education should look to the making of man, as man; that it should effectively assert the speculative as well as the practical exercise of intelligence; that it would be admirable to have a nation composed of men and women educated in the full intellectual tradition of the West and able to assume a constructive role in society. One might even agree that many universities are currently failing their task and "present themselves to our people in this crisis either as rather ineffectual trade schools or as places where nice boys and girls have a nice time under the supervision of nice men and women in a nice environment."[30] Many would agree, too, if the details were clarified, that education should, as Hutchins put it, draw out our common rational humanity rather than our individuality; that it should develop the capacity for constructive thinking; and that it is at least sensible to hope that philosophers and educators might reach some measure of consent on basic truths which have become the public property of all who can grasp evidence and arguments.

---

[30] Hutchins, *Education for Freedom*, pp. 25-26.

Nevertheless, when Hutchins and Adler elaborate these themes, they do seem, as their critics complain, to reduce human personality pretty much to intelligence alone and then to conceive intelligence itself in a manner too rationalistic and too static. They do appear to isolate the career of the mind from the rest of human life, from the total personality context, and from the existential facts of our human situation in history and in a universe which is one of change as well as one of stable factors. Time and again they speak as Adler does when he writes: "The direct product of liberal education is a good mind, well-disciplined in its processes of inquiring, and judging, knowing and understanding, and well furnished with knowledge, well-cultivated by ideas."[31] The intellectual accent is defensible enough, for Adler is talking of the university; and one does not wish to repeat the error of Newman's critics who obstinately charged the cardinal with ignoring the moral side of education because he maintained that promotion of intellectual values was the university's function. The difficulty here is rather with the overtones of this notion of an intelligence dealing with issues and ideas more or less divorced from the actual and historical settings in which alone all problems are posed. All this talk of clear ideas and positive convictions whereby, according to Hutchins, man cuts his way across the jungle of life seems on the one hand to make too little of the myriad personal and social factors, both conscious and unconscious, which influence men at every step. On the other hand this scheme of education seems to claim too much for abstract ideas themselves. One is perhaps reminded of St. Thomas' comment: "Life is an abstraction from

---

[31] Mortimer J. Adler, "Liberal Education—Theory and Practice," in *On General and Liberal Education: A Symposium,* p. 14 (Washington: Association for General and Liberal Education, 1945). Searching criticism of the Hutchins and Adler philosophy has been made by Robert Pollock, "President Hutchins and the Modern Problem of Education," *Jesuit Educational Quarterly* 4:182-92, March 1942.

something alive. The real aliveness of a living thing is its very being."[32]

"LABOR, LEISURE, AND LIBERAL EDUCATION"

When the Chicago plan was first announced it was also promptly denounced as antidemocratic. Its sponsors, as was observed, repudiated the charge on two counts. The education they advocated, they said, preserves and advances the well-being of democratic society by producing a thoughtful, self-reliant people able to see its own culture in historical perspective and to appreciate the past without worshiping it. Moreover, their program differed from Babbitt's, for instance, not only because its stress was on philosophy and science rather than on literature, but also because it had greatly widened the base of its clientele. More recently, in fact, it has aimed to encourage everybody to share in what Adler called the continuing task of adult education. By way of practical homage to the proposition that democracy requires universal liberal education, Hutchins and Adler guided a staff which produced in 1952 a set of *Great Books of the Western World*: seventy-four authors from Homer to Freud, in fifty-four volumes including Hutchins' introduction, *The Great Conversation*, and the *Syntopicon*, a two-volume topical index edited by Adler. The title of the set, said Hutchins pointedly, means some of the masterworks, not all. He hoped other editors would prepare a companion collection illustrating the eastern tradition, so that some day there might be a compilation of the Great Books of the World.

The collection is intended for the convenience of people reading privately or in discussion groups. It is not designed for a purely compensatory sort of adult education—correcting the deficiencies of the newly rich who aspire to dinner-table sparkle.

---

32 St. Thomas Aquinas, I *Contra gentes*, 98, in Thomas Gilby, translator, *St. Thomas Aquinas: Philosophical Texts*, p. 184. London: Oxford University Press, 1951.

Rather it is aimed at everyone, since liberal education ought to end only with life itself. Those who have never read the books will start and those who "took" them in college will now reread them maturely. For no college could have done more than prepare a man to educate himself later on when he seriously examines the issues of life and death facing civilization. The goals of such adult education are spacious indeed. For, as Hutchins sees it, the security of the future depends upon a world community of law and justice. Such a community, however, will only be the political expression of a more basic world republic of learning which enables the citizens of the globe to communicate with one another at the level of great ideas.

There are other aims which concern more immediately the individual and his private peace and happiness. It is hoped, for instance, that this liberal education nourished by the Great Books will help to humanize work and thereby resolve what Hutchins grants is one of the most baffling issues of our time. Work cannot be gotten rid of altogether, nor will the simple extension of leisure clear away all difficulties, for leisure trails a problem all its own, the problem of how to employ it profitably. Whoever hopes to besiege these questions successfully will do well, at the outset, to examine work itself and see how it fits into the over-all structure of life. In an essay on "Labor, Leisure, and Liberal Education" Adler finds the clue in a classic Aristotelian distinction which he restates with a difference.[33] It is not now to be in our democratic twentieth century a question of servile and liberal classes; but rather of a servile and liberal, or better, a leisure and a working, moment in every human life. For our activities are unequal in value. At the bottom of the scale are those biological operations which keep us alive; in the middle are the utilitarian efforts which on the one hand provide the roof and victuals which shelter and stoke the organism and

---

[33] Adler, "Labor, Leisure, and Liberal Education," p. 39.

on the other secure the leisure opportunity for those topmost, pre-eminently human pursuits of thinking, writing, reading, and religious contemplation. In this reckoning, work is a compulsory business and its worth lies in extrinsic compensations. Leisure activities, on the contrary, are desirable for their own sake, self-rewarding, and engaged in freely; for though they may be morally necessary, they are not physically so. Of course, the same activity may spring from different motives and consequently fall now into the category of work and now into that of leisure. Carpentry may be done for fun or money.

Adler underlines two errors to be avoided in any reflection about work: the aristocratic error of dividing men into laboring and leisure classes rather than dividing every man's life into a working and a leisure phase; and the industrial error which makes of work the only real good and which equates leisure with indolence or play. All right thinkers, however, will find the intelligible center in a true notion of leisure. Work will be understood as the purchase price of this leisure, while liberal education (including physical, moral, and intellectual training) is defined precisely as education for the good, the useful, and the noble employment of this same leisure.

This theory does not intend to exclude vocational training from the total educational picture. Its main target has rather been vocationalism, by which is meant devoting the time of the common schools to an actual induction into job methods, the tricks of the trade. Dewey, one recalls, was just as firm on this point and urged solid resistance to the pressures of those industrialists who would like to see the schools drill obedient automatons in routine skills. Hutchins adds that such training would be inefficient anyhow, since industry could always do it better, and unnecessary in the United States, where anyone who wants a job can get it! But it would be indefensible even were this not the case, for it distracts the school from its essential task of initiating youth into the civilization of reason. In that

civilizing effort Hutchins would not be willing to allot the instrumental method of shop and laboratory the same primacy Dewey
grants it, for he rejects the pragmatism which claims so much
for this process. It must be remembered, too, that Dewey had
the elementary school chiefly in mind, while Hutchins is concerned primarily with the education of college youth and adults
past college age. In fact, he once remarked that the elementary
schools were doing their work well enough.

Although he is opposed to vocationalism, Hutchins would
admit serious professional schools to the university for the education of the liberal-arts graduate. Such schools should aim, he
thinks, to develop the intellectual subject matter of those occupations which actually have a distinct theory underlying them:
medicine, law, divinity. The professional schools as presently
conducted are characteristically criticized when Hutchins up-
braids them for failing to transmit a systematic understanding
of the principles embodied in the work of the profession. Instead, time is wasted on the "anecdotal type" of instruction
which specializes in imparting helpful hints.[34] Aspiring beauticians and hotel managers would not be welcome in this university, for their techniques imply no learned theory. Hutchins
would have them trained in trade schools. This sort of suggestion infuriated Dewey, for it seemed to him a consignment of
this sort of vocational preparation to an academic ghetto. Break
down the dualism between the industrial and the cultural,
Dewey demanded, and give all children some understanding of
the scientific spirit concretized in work, for this is civilization's
most promising value. On the contrary, Hutchins would retort,
sustain that dualism and give all adults some understanding of
the philosophical and religious values which have shaped our

---

[34] For a statement of these ideas see Robert M. Hutchins, "The Place of Theological Education in a University," *Christian Education* 27:98-101, December
1943. In discussing here the role of a divinity school Hutchins provides a general summary of his views on the nature and aims of professional training.

culture, for these are the best treasures and the guarantees of all the rest.

Nevertheless Hutchins has not been satisfied with the purely extrinsic solution to the problem of work which says so simply that work is for the sake of leisure. In his introduction to the Great Books he does, indeed, repeat this crusty apothegm, but he has also been at some pains to show that the goal of liberal education is neither contrary to nor wholly apart from the life of work. It may not minister directly to that life, but neither is it designed to raise men above some fancied contamination by manual labor. Indeed, just as a liberal education equips men to exploit the richest possibilities of their leisure, so, too, it can make work itself more meaningful. For one thing, a great deal of this liberal education will be devoted to the physical and social sciences. These are part of the Great Conversation, says Hutchins as he makes his own Gilson's comment that our science is as much a part of our humanism as the science of Pericles' time was a part of Greek humanism. But if this is the case, a liberal education will help the industrial worker understand the mechanized processes of production and appreciate the social values of cooperative enterprise. These spacious suggestions, with their echo not only of Rousseau, Marx, and Dewey but of many opponents of naturalism as well, are generally, as we have noted, the hopeful comments of those who are not actually working in factories.

A worthwhile adult-education program will, moreover, engage people in the application of principles derived from their study to the problems they meet in their work. For if human labor is to be meaningful, it must be understood both in itself and in all its relationships. This, in turn, requires educated intelligences, intelligences nourished on the tradition of rational excellence represented by the Great Books. Hutchins, therefore, does not hesitate to say: "This set of books is offered not merely as an object upon which leisure may be expended, but also as a means to the humanization of work through understanding."[35] Of course, more than that is claimed for this liberal education. It promises to help men become wise, for without wisdom they can be neither happy nor good. It promises to educate them for the vocation of citizenship which, said Hutchins shortly after Hiroshima, is the vocational education the world needs.

The redemption of work and the flowering of leisure, individual self-possession and worldwide community—these are indeed splendid beacons. Whether the hopes they symbolize can be given substance by setting adult America tussling with all the questions raised for three thousand years by great thinkers and surrounded by them with countless affirmations and negations is at least doubtful. But the ambition itself commands respect.

---

[35] Hutchins, *The Great Conversation*, p. 16.

PART TWO

Elements of
a Christian Synthesis

CHAPTER V

The Dignity of Work
in Christian Thought*

Historians of technology cannot easily ignore Christianity, for the most striking advances in labor's prestige and productive power have originated in that western world so profoundly conditioned by the Christian faith. Moreover, as Carlton J. H. Hayes has remarked, the parallelism between a dynamic western civilization and a dynamic Christianity does not seem to be merely coincidental.[1] In cultures influenced, however falteringly, by the Christian ideals of mercy and fraternal charity technology has acquired, for instance, a new finality. Its genius has been expended, not on the tombs and terraced gardens of despots, but, by and large, on the effort to raise the general economic level. Doubtless there has been plenty of egoism and rapacity among Christians, but these vices are not peculiarly western. The really distinctive aspect of western progress is the one Professor Hayes points to: the way material gains have there been put to the service of humanitarian compassion. Nor has this interaction of the Christian inspiration and a civ-

---

* "And God pronounced his blessing on them, Increase and multiply and fill the earth, and make it yours. . . . So the Lord God took the man and put him in his garden of delight, to cultivate and tend it" (Genesis 1:28, 2:15).

[1] Carlton J. H. Hayes, *Christianity and Western Civilization*, pp. 46-50. Stanford: Stanford University Press, 1954.

ilization of work been a historical accident. There is good reason to argue that Christianity encloses a religious rationale motivating the technological development as well as the proper utilization of natural resources.

It should be noted at the outset that the Christian view of work is a center view. Its dominant feature, indeed, is precisely a balanced synthesis of those insights which acquire a more or less exclusive emphasis on the right and on the left. Consequently it will correspond at certain points with the aspirations of such disparate thinkers as Marx, Dewey, and Babbitt despite the radical cleavages between their over-all philosophies and Christianity. The Christian does not, for example, ground the specific dignity of man in his labor as Marxism does, but neither does he reduce work to its Hellenic status of a mere tool for the procurement of leisure. Christian educators will agree with Babbitt that manual labor is not the only sort of work and that the ethical effort at self-mastery is indeed crucial. Still, they may add that manual labor is the archetype, for after all, as Leo XIII wrote in *Rerum novarum*, there is no one who does not sustain life from what agriculture produces. And in any event the Christian is convinced that the necessary occupations of daily life can notably contribute, under the impact of grace, to ethical maturation itself. The Christian ideal, then, is neither Prometheus nor Plato. Marx is right, the Christian might say, in asking education to help men exploit the satisfactions of labor. Dewey is right when he underscores the significance of work as a powerful principle of community and educator of character or when he emphasizes the role of action for the full possession of certain truths. Nevertheless the concept of action is wider than the pragmatist is likely to admit and includes that contemplation which the humanists extol. The Christian will, therefore, defend a rhythm of work and reflection as the only adequate goal.

Consequently the ideal Christian humanist would embody both the creativity of technics and the immanent flowering of the inner life of the spirit. He would not defend any decisive divorce of the activities which transform the world from those which expand the individual, since their spheres are unified in the one human person. All work begins with a thought and a desire and it is consummated when these are concretized in the material wrought by a labor which both diminishes and fulfills the worker himself. Moreover, a man's religious experience, and indeed the whole of his intellectual and affective life, can and should have significant resonance in the zones of work and art. Though a Christian philosopher will not situate thought and muscular exertion on a strict continuum, neither will he rigidly compartmentalize the life of work and the life of the spirit. He will usually observe, instead, that man is neither purely *homo faber* nor exclusively *homo sapiens,* but a dynamic composite in which both aspects are mutually related and influential.

But just because this position is a center one, it is hard to maintain in practice. It is always so much easier to be extreme even in virtues. History will suggest, certainly, that the distinctively Christian ideal of labor has often been overclouded and that until rather lately Christian thinkers failed to exploit the idea itself as an antidote to the abuses dehumanizing work. It is a tragedy of our time, Maritain has remarked, that a primarily spiritual gain like the assertion of the dignity of work should have been linked during the past century with atheistic Marxism. It is similarly unfortunate that insights into the value of practical intelligence and into the role of social participation in the unfolding of personality should have been rather monopolized in America by various types of naturalism. For in such contexts these themes were often proposed so inaccurately that Christians were more concerned with refuting excesses than with recognizing perceptions that were actually honored by their own tradition.

Our present concern, however, is not with the negligences of Christians nor with the cartoons of their adversaries, but rather with the authentic Christian concept of work and its worth, especially as it has been elaborated in contemporary Catholic thought.[2] In recent decades there has been a great deal of discussion focused on these topics and it has issued in areas both of agreement and controversy. There is agreement, for instance, on the unacceptability of all extreme solutions. In the same way that Christian social thought rejects both an excessive individualism and an excessive collectivism, so its humanists reject both that static speculation which Eric Gill called false angelism and that frenzied commitment to unrelieved technology which critical Europeans sometimes claim that they have discovered in the United States.

It would be agreed, too, that work is a means, since all labor has interwoven with it a strain toward the future. For Christians, however, it is not merely labor but life itself which has a basically instrumental and futuristic character. Naturalism, of course, would not quarrel with the instrumentalist accent as such. It, too, admits that a lively sense of futures does unify the vital forces and give them forward impulse. It is rather the character and the location of the religious goal which the naturalist finds intolerable—as when, for example, a Leo XIII will write:

> The things of earth cannot be understood or valued aright without taking into consideration the life to come, the life that will know no death. Exclude the idea of futurity, and forthwith the very notion of what is good and right would perish; nay, the whole scheme of the universe would become a dark and unfathomable mystery.[3]

---

[2] An excellent introduction to the genuine Catholic view of temporal realities and culture is to be had in the notable collection of brief extracts from the writings of Pius XII, in Robert C. Pollock, editor, *The Mind of Pius XII* (New York: Crown Publishers, 1955).

[3] Leo XIII, *Rerum novarum*, quoted here from the translation, "Rights and Duties of Capital and Labor," in Etienne Gilson, editor, *The Church Speaks to the Modern World: The Social Teachings of Leo XIII*, p. 216. New York: Doubleday and Company, 1954.

Catholicism, however, blends with its futurism a fundamental, logical esteem of the present moment and of the work done therein. It does this, in fact, much more successfully than either Marxism or pragmatism because it points up more convincingly the intrinsic values, both natural and sacramental, of the very act of working and thereby enhances rather than dehydrates the significance of *now*. For a religious man work has a greater significance than it could have as a pure tool building civilizations and securing our tomorrows. Like every truly human action, work, for the Christian, implicates a moral choice as it unfolds; and it is in his work that a man either effectively commits himself to or turns aside from the fulfillment of the divine design in his regard.

A certain diversity of opinion does appear among Christian writers, however, once they begin to inquire more closely into the precise nature of work values. No one doubts that human labor is both natural and necessary, and hence neither ignoble nor dispensable. The human collectivity as a whole, at least, is compelled to work for its sustenance, and even the rich man may find himself indirectly obliged to work in order to avoid the snares of indolence or fulfill his responsibilities to the common welfare. The prudent administration of a great fortune may be toilsome enough. Nevertheless it can still be asked whether the benefits of work are limited to these obvious instrumental and ascetical purposes. Is there any authentic value in all that brilliant extrapolation of technology which goes so far beyond the mere provision of life's necessities and the discipline of wayward impulses? Theologians will quickly point out that this is only the specific phase of a more general inquiry into the religious meaning of human history; that is to say, into the worth of human events and civilizations in the light of transtemporal goals. This, in turn, is itself a particularization of the most fundamental question of all, the problem of the relationship between nature and grace, between our natural perspectives and capacities and the supernatural destiny which invades and everywhere transforms them.[4]

Work and its fruits, especially modern mechanized production, are instances of those "terrestrial realities," as continental writers like to call them, whose value relative to salvation is not altogether clear. A rather negative view is taken of such work on practical grounds by certain hardheaded debunkers and on dogmatic grounds by those theologians of history who are sometimes called eschatologists because they accent the absolute transcendence and dominance of the kingdom of God, man's last end, and consequently disparage secular human action since it is incapable in itself of ever achieving that kingdom. The practical critics attack contemporary developments and argue, for instance, that machinism neither increases leisure nor renders society more rational. On the contrary, they say, it chains men to a debasing servitude, for the wheels must be kept incessantly spinning and leisure employed in feverish consumption lest the machines slow down. Sometimes the ambiguities of that economy of abundance which work expands are underlined, and it is charged that sensuality and egoism are being nourished on a national scale. When these critics turn their attention to the reflective efforts aimed at Christianizing work, they ask destructively just why work is supposed to be so holy anyhow. See how unchristian the factory milieu and its labor force actually are, they object. Do you really think you can purify either? Men work to survive. Let us not pretend that their occupation is a vocation. It should be permeated by faith in some fashion, but even this seems impossible if a man has chosen his job for egocentric reasons or if it produces only goods or services which in no way further society's real interests.

---

[4] This is a theme elaborated by, among others, M. -D. Chenu, *Pour une théologie du travail* (Paris: Editions du Seuil, 1955) and L. Malevez, "Deux théologies catholiques de l'histoire," *Bijdragen* 10:225-40, 1949.

It is no accident, perhaps, that criticisms of this sort are more frequently voiced by Protestants than by Catholics.[5] Luther's theology of work did indeed, as Max Weber pointed out, bestow the aura of a special vocation on the ordinary employments of life. Its sanctification of labor was a Protestant commonplace even after the rest of Lutheran theology had been discarded. But it claimed rather too much and some reaction was probably inevitable. The author who makes the charges summarized here says that, when he told Emil Brunner the hoary anecdote about the diverse aims of three men working on a cathedral, Brunner remarked that he would prefer to be the second man, emphasizing the wages which would support his family. Apparently, the third laborer's claim to be working for God seemed to the Swiss theologian somewhat pretentious.

The Catholic eschatologist might agree with Brunner. At least, he would not be surprised by the evidence which suggests that modern advances in technical culture corrupt rather than ennoble man, for he already knows that no amount of civilizing effort will transform earth into the true paradise. He will readily grant that human work has a religious value, but will add that this is in no way proportioned to the natural brilliance or power of the work itself but only to the interior spirit of faith and charity which activates the worker. Thus Thérèse of Lisieux washing handkerchiefs in the convent laundry was, in terms of supernatural values, working more effectively than the most gifted artist or engineer motivated by exclusively self-regarding, temporal aims. The eschatologist is not, therefore, inclined to bother much about work's intrinsic worth, since he is more impressed by its fundamental impotency where spiritual ends are concerned.

---

[5] See Sherwood Eliot Wirt, "Is Work So Holy?" *Christian Century* 73:995-96, August 29, 1956. A Catholic critique in somewhat similar vein is voiced by Lawrence Moran, "The Myth of Machine-Made Leisure," *Social Order* 6:434-39, November 1956.

A more positive view is taken by the temperamentally optimistic as well as by those theologians whose fundamental attitude is sometimes called incarnationist because they are particularly inspired with the thought that the incarnation of the Word has sanctified not only human nature, but all its admirable cultural manifestations. They do not, of course, deny that grace and salvation come wholly from God's merciful bounty, but they also believe that the progressive civilization both of individuals and society does, in a way, prepare the natural soil to benefit most fully from the impact of the divine gift. Whether a field is cultivated or not, writes Father Truhlar in a discussion of the relationship between human gifts and the spiritual life, has no effect on the sun, which shines according to its own laws. "But once the sun is shining, it makes a great deal of difference whether the field is cultivated or uncultivated."[6]

Now, the development of technology ideally involves a parallel development of the workers' own intellectual powers and total personality. Moreover, it results in a betterment of life's natural quality and conditions, and this itself influences behavior since, as St. Thomas observed, some degree of material security is necessary for the consistent practice of virtue. When a plague like ringworm was mastered, for instance, whole communities in the American South were rescued from a degenerative listlessness. The incarnationist is not at all prepared to grant that modern technical culture has a generally corrupting effect. By and large, he argues, it has given the people of the West the chance to be fully human, and this itself disposes them, though not with any ineluctable necessity, for the action of grace. Even the argument from the actual abuses is, in a sense, irrelevant. For if industrialization does not really increase gen-

---

[6] C. Truhlar, "Human Nature and the Spiritual Life," *Theology Digest* 5:35, Winter 1957. The original text, "De viribus naturae humanae in vita spirituali," appeared in *Gregorianum* 35:608-29, 1954.

uine leisure, at least it could do so and the fact that it does not is due to other and more perennial weaknesses. If the industrial environment is often degrading, still it is not so by any inherent and irreversible force. The incarnationist believes, moreover, that divine grace itself inspires mankind to a progressive technical mastery of physical forces. For on the one hand, as Père Malevez remarks, this natural perfection seems to be in some way connected with the proper accomplishment of grace's own function in individual souls because it helps to dispose them for its effects. And on the other hand, history itself strains to see the spirit of Christ penetrate ever more fully all human institutions and products. It is, therefore, the duty of Christians to bring art and science, work and technology, politics and economics within the beneficent ambit of the Redeemer.

It will be clear enough that the Christian defense of work's dignity finds more resources in the thought of the incarnationists than in that of the eschatologists. It might be remarked, too, that, while the eschatological theme is struck by Protestant theologians as well as by distinguished Catholic ones, the incarnationist accent is most often formulated by Catholics—although, doubtless, the average American Protestant layman shows no tendency to depreciate "terrestrial realities." In these pages we simply gather together some of the main points made by Catholic writers reflecting on human labor, leaving to the final chapter the application of these themes to Christian education. It was remarked earlier that the geographical provenance of the material is worth notice. For most of the essays on the philosophy of work or its theology, on the need to restore its joys and reassert its dignity, are by Europeans and particularly by French writers. Here in America there has not been much urge to defend the prestige of work in theory, since it is adequately acknowledged in practice. For a French theologian, schooled as he is in a tradition which is peculiarly national, it may be something of a novelty to challenge the notion that men work simply to live, but Americans customarily recognize that this is by no means the main motivation in many concrete cases, even though it may have some logical or historical priority. It is easily acknowledged that work fulfills other drives—for creative expression, for status, for service, or for the effective sublimation of threatening impulses.

Not infrequently, to be sure, Europeans charge that Americans have only a technical, not a sapiential, culture. And perhaps the past four centuries devoted to mastering and making habitable a rich, unbroken continent have had their negative side. But they have also provided sapiential rewards of their own. As Barbara Ward, a wise and sympathetic British observer, wrote warmly:

> Yet to be concerned with material things is not of itself a sign that culture is lacking. On the contrary, a large proportion of the measurements of culture are based on material objects—architecture, furniture, materials, pottery. . . . Can anyone doubt that, in the central position in American society—in short, in the American home—the effort to improve, to simplify, to make more beautiful and more functional does not amount to what would be called, if prejudice were less, a cultural effort? . . . There is, moreover, a factor in this American culture of the home which, by any standard, should give it a higher social value. It is that so much of it is done by husband and wife in overalls, paint brush and glue pot in hand, working to the plan they have puzzled out together.
>
> For so many people abroad—especially in the hotter, lazier continents—the American way of life appears to have come down, in some vast cornucopia, from heaven. What is not measured is the steadiness and the intensiveness of the work which sustains it all. . . .
>
> If work, disciplined, steady work, is "materialism," then, certainly, the Americans are materialists but it is the oldest wisdom of Europe that "to work is to pray."[7]

---

[7] Barbara Ward, "Report to Europe on America." *New York Times Magazine,* pp. 47-48, June 20, 1954.

It is possible that certain thoughtful European Christians have felt that too exclusive a preoccupation with literary, philosophical, or political speculation leaves the Marxists in solitary possession of the theoretical defense of work and technology. At any rate, under whatever influence, they have produced stimulating studies of those work values which Americans honor effectively indeed, but unreflectively. The significance of these studies, however, is universal, for theory is never safely disregarded for long. After all, Americans also confront the problems raised by modern industrialized work and they cannot apply a Christian solution if they do not know it. A Belgian theologian writing on the Catholic sense of work will remark deprecatingly that his enterprise is unoriginal. In this country, however, it is not uncommon to find reputable authors imputing to Christianity a view of labor quite opposed to its actual position and imagining that in the Christian tradition work is simply a penalty of original sin.

The total Catholic view of work, like the Catholic theory of education and of economics, has twin sources, since the complete illumination of any natural phenomenon requires the light both of reason and of revelation. Man's labor is a concrete reality in the world as we know it and the full Christian concept of work's character and function will include, not contradict, a sound human analysis. In his Christmas Eve discourse of 1953 Pius XII several times used the phrase "il concetto umano e cristiano de lavoro—the human and Christian concept of work," as if to suggest this basic agreement. At the same time, the full religious significance of work, its ultimate finality and spiritual worth, cannot be grasped apart from the perspectives opened up by Christ. Metaphysics will analyze labor abstractly. The theological study of work does not, in its turn, envision an intrinsically different sort of object, but it does examine its meaning in the real world, divinely created and profoundly affected by the disobedience of the first Adam and the obedience of the second.

Faith teaches the Christian that his labor is instrumental at a level unknown to philosophy. For since it is understood and willed, it is a moral act and therefore directly significant in that economy of salvation which involves man's ethical response through grace to the challenges of life. Thus work falls within the purview of theology, the science that extends to all that has bearing upon salvation and to all supernatural values, as well as to the natural ones which minister to them.

Nowadays we are aware that every man has two aspects, two functions, two sides to himself: the individual and the social. These are reciprocal but not identical, distinct yet not separate, since it is one and the same worker, for instance, whose substantial being is incommunicable but whose toil is inescapably social in origin and effect. Few human activities, indeed, so clearly implicate at one and the same time the development of the individual personality and the development of social life as does work. When the Christian thinker, therefore, studies labor, he not only submits it to the twofold scrutiny of philosophy and theology, but he examines in each case both its individual and its social dimension. The total view of human work which emerges from these inquiries has three strands. There is the philosophical thread which amounts to a rational penetration of the object by careful reflection on the data of experience supplemented by relevant insights from the behavioral sciences. There is the theological penetration of work's religious meaning through reflection upon the implications and interrelationships of revealed truths. There is, finally, the integration of this rounded concept of work into the over-all fabric of the Christian understanding of life. For work is not the whole of that life but one factor which must be harmonized with others.

THE NATIVE DIGNITY OF WORK

The late Pius XII was to a remarkable degree concerned with calling men's attention to the religious dimension of their temporal action and his characteristic comment on technology and its fruits provides us here with a lapidary text:

> The Church loves and favors human progress. . . . "Inhabit the earth and subject it" (*Gen.* 1, 28) said God to man as He handed creation over to him in temporary heritage.[8]

When the Christian philosopher analyzes work as a real element in the real world, he arrives at two conclusions which are of interest here. In the first place, he observes that work is a natural function and not a mere penal necessity. But since this is so, one is not surprised to find that it is more than just a meal ticket and is, in fact, a genuine humanizing force which actuates individual and social potentialities. It is worthwhile asking what sort of work best fits this description. In contemporary western civilization we are accustomed, for instance, to distinguish work which produces goods from that which produces services. In 1956, in fact, the number of Americans employed in the production of things on farms, in factories, mines, or the building trades was actually less than the number employed in all other activities. Some of these other activities, however, do exemplify the notion of craftsmanship, and the skilled chef or auto mechanic is close in his creativity to the class of goods producers.

The production of goods itself sustains distinctions of degree according to whether or not it is highly industrialized and mechanical. In some types of manual labor men are little more than wheels and levers supplying energy, and this is far from the splendid productivity of the artist or the inventor. On the other hand, there are certain magnificent accomplishments like driving vehicular tunnels through river beds or erecting noble bridges and buildings which are precisely the effect of a collectivity—a laboring giant made up of the united efforts of many men. Some of these may perform individually operations of a

---

[8] Pius XII, "Christmas Eve Address: 1953," pp. 175-76.

rather simple or routine sort. Even so, their situation is quite
different from that of a factory worker making part of a hat.
For it is not impossible that one person should make a whole
hat, but no one man could achieve the triumphant engineering
projects which add so much both to the beauty and the efficiency
of our cities. These are stirring testimonials to the unique power
of cooperative labor.

Nevertheless the work which most fully corresponds to the
philosophical analyses is probably the sort associated with the
image of the independent craftsman or the family farmer. For
in its archetypal form work is commonly said to represent the
embodiment of an idea in matter and as such it is, remarks Père
Chenu, an activity peculiarly proper to man, who is himself an
incarnate spirit. Out of a block of wood the cabinetmaker fashions a chest; out of some acres of underbrush the husbandman
makes a truck garden. An idea in the worker's mind has been
realized in the objective order and nature has been humanized.

Of course, the term *work* can be correctly applied to a rich
profusion of activities and is certainly analogous. There are,
for instance, the conventional categories of manual and intellectual labor, each divided and subdivided into thousands of
types and blends. If they can all be called work, they must be
alike in some respect; and St. Thomas, in fact, was able to sub-
sume both physical and intellectual occupations under a single
rubric. For the university lecturer toils for his sustenance even
as the farmer does, and so his labor is manual, too, since, says
Thomas, "By manual labor we understand not only what is done
by hand . . . but, briefly, any occupation whereby a man earns
his living."[9] This is, to be sure, a rather specialized use of the

---

[9] St. Thomas Aquinas, "De opere manuali," *Quodlibet VII*, a. 17, c. The same point
is made in *Summa theologica*, IIa IIae, q. 187, a. 3, c. Articles 17 and 18 of
Quodlibet VII constitute the *Quaestio disputata de opere manuali*. A modern
edition is to be had in R. P. Mandonnet, editor, *S. Thomae Aquinatis quaestiones quodlibetales*, pp. 280-96 (Paris: P. Lethielleux, 1926).

label and a rather sharp concentration on the economic function, for there are other links between the two categories. Just as there operate in the artisan both the skillful hand and the directive intelligence, so in the community itself the work of the research scientist, the administrator, educator, or social expert, is found developing and ameliorating the conditions of production or guiding and strengthening the social structure which manual labor supports and within which its energies unroll. In *Rerum novarum*, Leo XIII observes that every citizen should contribute to the common good. Still, the contributions will vary, and he assigns a place of honor to the legislators, jurists, executives, and soldiers who do "the work of the commonwealth" because their labor is so intimately linked with the community's collective interests. But this is not to depreciate the toil of farmers, tradesmen, engineers, and artisans, whose work is, said the pope, "so important that it may be truly said that it is only by the labor of workingmen that states grow rich."

Again, a Thomist like Yves Simon can make Babbitt's point about ethical work more cogently than Babbitt himself did. Simon shows convincingly that the intelligent effort to put rational order into the sphere of human appetites, both in oneself and in society, is correctly labeled *moral work*. For, like manual labor and technical thinking, this is a useful activity and presupposes a world in process where improvements and restorations are possible. Only here, it is responsible freedom that is aimed at rather than mastery of physical forces.[10] Of course, it may happen that a man is simultaneously engaged in physical and moral work, in the production of things and in the formation of his own character. For the farmer who disciplines himself to perseverance under the pitiless sun reaps more than fodder for his cattle.

---

[10] Yves Simon, "The Concept of Work," in Robert B. Heywood, editor, *The Works of the Mind*, pp. 6-7. Chicago: The University of Chicago Press, 1947.

Granting all these distinctions, one may go on to ask the Christian philosopher how he understands this manifold enterprise of work, particularly that which produces goods. It is, we are told, a decisive example of that human activity through objects which so impressed Marx. For in manual labor a man comes to grips with the world of things as he operates on and through them. This is, moreover, an eminently connatural activity, as St. Thomas argues in one of the *Quaestiones quodlibetales*. An examination of men's physical structure, he points out, shows them to be naturally oriented toward manual work. The lower animals, for their part, are adequately equipped from birth to sustain life. Their food is within reach; their hides and fur protect them and tooth and claw defend. In place of these natural granaries and arsenals men have two unique instruments: the hand and the mind. They can, therefore, take thought for their needs and devise and wield the complex, artificial tools which execute their designs.[11]

When St. Thomas speaks of work, he generally has its utilitarian aims uppermost in mind, although he acknowledges others which indicate that work is not only a natural exigency but also a natural fulfillment. Pius XI accented these latter aspects when he observed that God has given us a wealth of natural resources whose development implies a concomitant expansion of personality. "What else is work but the application of one's forces of soul and body to these gifts of nature for the development of one's powers by their means?"[12] Christian thought, in fact, like many other theories of labor, distinguishes two related effects of work: its humanization of nature and its education of man. Scholastic terminology sums up this distinction of two finalities with the phrases *perfectio operantis* and *perfectio*

---

[11] St. Thomas Aquinas, "De opere manuali," a. 17, c.

[12] Pius XI, *Quadragesimo anno*, quoted here from *Encyclical Letter of Pope Pius XI on Reconstructing the Social Order*, p. 15. New York: Paulist Press, 1939.

operis. A Darwinian behaviorism will distrust this division on the grounds that it breaks up the perfect continuity of organism and environment. For this theory would like to see no other "perfection of the agent" than the activity itself which the proper stimulus can always cue. The Christian philosopher, however, while acknowledging that these two perfections are engendered by the same activity and are vitally interrelated, believes that careful analysis shows to be really distinct the physical operation fashioning a table, the perfection acquired by a block of wood which becomes a piece of handsome furniture, and the satisfaction and increase of skill which the worker acquires and retains after his work is over.

Descriptions of work will vary somewhat as one or another of these finalities monopolizes the writer's attention. The monopoly is never total, of course. Even if one emphasizes products, one can still see that work fulfills the worker. Howsoever it be explained, it is clear enough that a skilled stonemason is more fully alive after he has mastered his craft than when he was in apprenticeship. When the work activity itself is the focus of attention, no doubt the transformation of matter will seem primary. For unlike contemplation, which is an immanent activity perfecting the thinker himself, manual labor is transient and issues in the first place in a benefit for the material wrought. It is for this reason that Yves Simon profoundly observes that all work has an aspect of generosity in the pure metaphysical line, since the workman enriches an object exterior to himself.[13] This humanization of nature, as suggested, is possible precisely in virtue of those spiritual attributes of freedom and intelligence which distinguish men from beasts. The worker, in the first place, concocts his plan and wills its execution. We saw that Marx also recognized this distinctive moment of design, preparation, and intention, but the exigencies of his philosophy

---

[13] Yves Simon, *Trois leçons sur le travail*, p. 2. Paris: Pierre Tequi, 1938.

would not permit him to see here a revelation of the uniquely human factor even though he knew that it was just this conscious forecast which bees and spiders lack. In the second place, the worker reproduces this model in the material at hand: in wood or iron, in the soil or on canvas, in the organization of a factory or the presentation of a lesson to a class. He concretizes the form first engendered by his own spirit. And so, wrote Leo XIII, when the farmer "turns the activity of his mind and the strength of his body toward procuring the fruits of nature, by such an act he makes his own that portion of nature's field which he cultivates—that portion on which he leaves, as it were, the impress of his personality."[14]

If one agrees with St. Thomas that art in the radical sense is the power of making things properly, one will easily see a basic continuity between all skillful work and the so-called fine arts. Not every product, of course, qualifies as artistic, but any well-wrought work deserves that title: the furniture of fine lines, the functional and graceful bridge, the successful cake or the shoe nicely repaired. For these productions are not the result of chance but of an abiding intellectual value which insures consistently successful production. A craftsman as such, says St. Thomas, "is commendable not for the will with which he does a work, but for the quality of the work. Art, therefore, properly speaking is an operative habit."[15] Until his death in 1940 the English artist Eric Gill was a vigorous and eloquent publicist for this thesis. His books, as he frankly owned, all preached this theme even as his life as a draftsman, designer of type faces, worker in stone and wood loyally exemplified it. He liked to

---

[14] Leo XIII, "Rights and Duties of Capital and Labor," p. 209. In this fact of the humanization of material things through work the pope sees a natural argument supporting some private ownership of property.

[15] St. Thomas Aquinas, *Summa theologica*, Ia IIae, q. 57, a. 3, c. The translation is from *The Summa Theologica of St. Thomas Aquinas*, translated by the Fathers of the English Dominican Province, Vol. 7, pp. 90-91.

echo the phrase of the Indian philosopher Ananda Coomar-swamy: "The artist is not a special kind of man, but every man is a special kind of artist." The obverse of this enthusiasm was, rather inevitably, a pessimistic view of modern industrialism. Gill could not see how factory work is ever to be pervaded by the satisfactions of art so long as workers do not set their own goals or execute more than a fraction of the project. For the artist must be the craftsman deliberately making well the whole product he has himself envisioned. No doubt this indictment is justified in part, although it is not clear that the notion of art is quite unverified in the corporate efforts of a team of workers jointly turning out a handsome car. But even if it is true that genuine technical culture is impossible under mechanization, still the school is capable of guarding the ideal of craftsmanship, for its concern is naturally with humanistic values rather than with industrial efficiency or mass output.

The notion of art as an abiding intellectual perfection, an ontological enlargement of the artist, underlines again that second finality of work, its characteristic perfecting of the worker himself. When a man toils, he is implicated in a congeries of activities not all of which enrich merely the external product. For his own skill grows by intelligent exercise and so do his prudence and wisdom, his courage and patience. He ponders, tests, and checks. He knows the joy, as Jean Lacroix said, of bringing true values to life both in himself and in the matter which he transforms. These humanistic values of labor also include its potential as ethical educator and as a factor developing the social capacity in man. When it is said that work, besides being a source of aesthetic satisfaction and a progenitor of intellectual and bodily skills, also cultivates such moral qualities as steadiness, responsibility, and generosity, it is a question, certainly, of the ideal. It is granted that under brutal conditions just the opposite results may be obtained. This may partly explain the fondness which Christian tradition shows for the work of the self-sufficient farmer. St. Thomas would delight modern agrarians when he writes in his commentary on the *Politics* that the soundest republic is the one whose citizens are mostly engaged in agriculture. The rhythm of their constant, balanced work preserves them from mischievous idleness, while its steady satisfactions make of them a people who can elect and correct their leaders without themselves burning for excessive personal honors.[16] This theme is echoed in a message which Pius XII sent in 1954 to the National Catholic Social Life Conference in Canada. For as he praised the dignity of the life of those who work the land, the pope counseled the Canadian farmer not easily to abandon his calling for the disillusionments of the city.

But the virtues predicated of the rural worker are, no doubt, required in some form or other of all men and every métier can contribute to their nurture. Any work, for example, obliges a man to submit to a law, to conform to the nature of the medium and consent to its discipline. It is true, as Rudolf Allers points out, that games also have their rules, but these are man-made and can be changed when we like. In work, however, reality lays down the laws and the workmen must abide by its prescriptions.[17] More than seventy-five years ago Felix Adler, founder of the Ethical Culture Schools, was remarking that manual work instills a sense of rightness and respect for honest workmanship, for in this sphere poor work cannot pass muster. Thomists like Maritain and Simon, speaking from the standpoint of quite a different philosophy, make the same observation. Simon points out that, though a brilliant decor may win fame for a shoddy metaphysics, there is no praise for a key which won't open the

---

[16] For a selection of pertinent Thomistic texts and references see Sylvester Michael Killeen, *The Philosophy of Labor According to Thomas Aquinas*, pp. 63-64 (Washington: The Catholic University of America Press, 1939).

[17] Rudolf Allers, *Character Education in Adolescence*, pp. 157-59. New York: Joseph F. Wagner, 1940.

door. And one is reminded of the remark made by Charles **F.** Kettering, the American inventor: "It's easy to build a philosophy. It doesn't have to run."

There is considerable significance in all this for school practice. We are reminded that education for the common human vocation of work is by no means limited to professional or technical training nor to shops and garden projects. Young people are inducted into the authentic spirit of work when they take up seriously a demanding study: mathematics, a language, science, philosophy. The rules of these matters must be respected; one cannot improvise at will. French grammar, geometry, the technique of the laboratory and the well-established conclusions of the sciences or of exact philosophical reflection—all these require not only personal action for personal appropriation but also a docility which moderates the free flow of subjectivity, an obedience to the conditions of the object, a respect for the methods of sound work. And here, at least, we should be able to count on transfer, since a conscious appreciation of this basic law of labor has a universal import; it already reaches out to all forms of work.

This awareness of and submission to the law of work also serves to make intelligible the struggle so often accompanying our occupations. Jean Lacroix has indicated how natural such struggle is, since in work the human spirit seeks to penetrate and transform nature and this is not done without strenuous exercise. Moreover, laborious effort is also an inevitable companion of intellectual and ethical work, for one does not master science, or grasp profound truths, or organize one's own behavior rationally save by militant and persevering toil.[18]

The Christian analysis of morality does not, as we know, equate goodness with social effectiveness nor make the community itself the ultimate aim and sanction of a noble life. Never-

18 Jean Lacroix, "La notion de travail." *La Vie Intellectuelle* 20:7-8, June 1952.

theless it recognizes very clearly the interpersonal character of
life and much virtuous action. Our whole being is oriented toward others and our ethical life is resumed in that law of charity
which points to our central relationships to God and to our fellow men. A great deal of our conscious activity is inescapably
social in character and most ethical imperatives are simply designed to expedite the reign of a community of brotherhood. We
know, too, that growth in the Christian life means growth in that
spirit of altruism, which, as St. Paul told the Philippians,
prompts each one to look not to his own interests but to those of
others. It is not surprising, then, that Christian thinkers point
out, as do many others, how work contributes to the construction
of society and the strengthening of fraternal spirit. For one
thing, labor lays those material bases of society—for example,
transportation and communication systems—without which men
would not become fully social in fact. Even more importantly,
work helps weave the first spiritual bonds of community and
powerfully instructs the individual in appreciation of social
values.[19] For when men work together and share the experience
of a common toil with all its anxieties, perils, and rewards, they
discover one another, as Père Bovis puts it, and fraternization
begins, if not fraternity. Work, indeed, is the pre-eminent mode
of cooperative activity. No one really toils in isolation; and to
produce goods whose significance almost always stems from
their relevance in social life is to recognize one's own social nature. There are obvious and precious insights here for the educator. We talk a great deal about the value of sports, which in

---

[19] This is an observation made by almost all who write on the humanistic values of
work. See, for writers working from the varying perspectives of psychology
and theology, Rudolf Allers, *The Psychology of Character*, translated by E. B.
Strauss, p. 136 (New York: Sheed and Ward, 1939) and André de Bovis,
"Le sens catholique du travail et de la civilisation," *Nouvelle Revue Théologique* 72:365-66, April 1950. This study is concluded in the May number of
the same periodical, pp. 468-78.

fact generally pit students against one another. We might do well to think more carefully of those work projects which call upon us to unite our efforts and incarnate them in an achievement which lasts after the work is over as a silent witness to our common aspiration.

There is one more element in the philosophical analysis of work which needs to be mentioned if only to forestall an objection. For when we speak of work projects in the school, it may be said that these are not properly labor because they lack that note of gritty necessity which marks true adult work. No doubt a study of work is incomplete without reference to motives. The banker who pities the ditchdigger may spend his own holiday spading the garden. The physical operation is the same in both cases though it is called toil in one and recreation in the other. The activity of work must, therefore, be seen in what Yves Simon called its ethicosocial context. In that context, this Thomist philosopher who has carefully examined the whole idea of work is able to distinguish it clearly both from play and from the strenuous but illegal business of thieves and smugglers. Work, he observes, is always an instance of the fulfillment of some law. It is an activity obedient to some precept of biological or rational nature, of natural or social authority, of professional or social status or religious obligation. It is not, therefore, limited to what is done for economic gain. A doctor who works gratuitously is still fulfilling the obligations of charity and of his profession. This characteristic distinguishes labor in the strict sense both from toilsome hobbies which lie outside the corral of duty, however beneficial they may be, and from activities ethically invalid. The efforts of the housebreaker, Simon comments, are only ironically denominated "work." Men commonly reserve that honorable term for employment whose aim and circumstances are morally good.[20]

---

[20] Simon, *Trois leçons sur le travail*, pp. 14-17.

These distinctions, significant as they are, do not mean that the activities of a school shop, a hobby club, or a work project are unrelated to a humanism of work. The school is interested, to be sure, in work activities rather than work in the strict sense suggested above. It is interested, though, not only because it seeks to cultivate certain distinctive values of creativeness and cooperativeness in the young student here today. It is interested also because it wants to accustom him to find satisfaction in and accept the rigors of that "real" work which will be his tomorrow. To this end, as we shall say more fully later, the ideal education would provide young people with a practical experience of work as well as with an understanding of its nature and dignity. Such an understanding, though, is complete only when man's labor is seen in the religious perspective which reveals its fullest stature.

THE RELIGIOUS ASPECTS OF WORK

The Christian theology of work both reinforces and supplements the insights of sound philosophy. Using its own resources, it confirms, for instance, the idea of the native dignity of labor, a theme suggested in the very first verses of the Bible. For in those mysterious lines God Himself is shown engaged in a creation which has analogous similarities to work although it implies no change, fatigue, or struggle in the divine artificer. Moreover, human work itself is revealed here as something always quite natural, though not always dolorous. For when the mists lifted over the earth and the waters receded from the land, the innocent first man receives two commissions charting the rhythm of action and contemplation in his life. He is commanded by God to work, to cultivate and develop the plantation of Eden, and he is also charged with the naming of the animals. But this latter duty symbolized his contemplative function, for among ancient peoples to name things was to know them as they are in themselves.

This tableau from Genesis which shows us Adam concerned with work even before his disobedience was touched upon obliquely by Pius XI when he remarked in *Quadragesimo anno* that physical labor "was decreed by Providence for the good of man's body and soul even after original sin"—so much the more, then, before that sin. In his apostolic constitution *Sponsa Christi*, which treats of the life of contemplative nuns, Pius XII wrote:

> All, not excepting men and women engaged in the contemplative life, are under an obligation to work, whether with their minds or with their hands, and this obligation is not only of natural law but it is a duty of penance and satisfaction. Besides, labor is a general instrument for preserving the mind from danger and raising it to higher things. By it we cooperate as we ought in the work of divine Providence, both natural and supernatural, and perform works of charity.[21]

The Christmas Eve discourse of 1953, which we have quoted before, underlined this notion of work's religious significance with some striking phrases. For although the pope criticized that idolatry of work which constitutes "the technological spirit," he also praised modern industrial and technical conquest: "machines and numbers, laboratories and inventions, power and resources." Such progress, he declared, comes from God and should lead to Him. When offered to the Creator it constitutes, in fact, the fulfillment of the directive given in the garden at the dawn of time.

An esteem for work is naturally bound up with the Christian view of material creation. For if the elements which technology exploits have value, so also has this process which properly develops them. A Belgian theologian, Père André de Bovis, has pointed to some of the documents in which the Church proclaims

---

21 Pius XII, "Sponsa Christi," quoted here from the translation, "The Bride of Christ," in *Life of the Spirit* 6:224, December 1951. The original text is in *Acta Apostolicae Sedis* 43:5-24, January 10, 1951.

the inherent goodness of the tangible world. The professions of faith, for example, indicate the base of this insight when they celebrate God as the Creator of both the heavens and the earth. Matter is not spirit, but it does come equally from the hand of God, all of whose works are good. Consequently, in the first centuries of our era, various local councils denounced extreme detractors of things material. The Second Council of Braga anathematized the Priscillians, who had taught that human souls were exiled in bodies because of some sin committed in a previous heavenly dwelling and who spoke genially of the *creatio universae carnis* as the *opificium* of the devils. But as Père Bovis remarks, Christianity has never had any part with such fantasies nor with those oriental systems which despise the supposedly opaque being of the world even as contemporary forms of Sartrean existentialism have done. On the contrary, for Christians the natural relationship between man born to be an artisan and the material world which awaits his touch is one of amity rather than hostility. Nature is not thought of as a half-benign, half-malevolent force with which men must struggle. It is seen, instead, within the perspective of creation and the incarnation and it is believed that, since the world comes from God, its least and lowest elements bespeak Him. Besides, at the incarnation the whole universe acquired a sacramental aura as the Word assumed a body made from earth and employed the products of the soil—bread, oil, and wine—as channels of His grace.[22]

This outlook does not promote any giddy optimism. Christians know that work involves painful effort if natural resources are to be developed. But this very effort aims to render nature more rational and more friendly, and is not really a conflict between two enemies. Work humanizes the earth in a movement which is, to use Lacroix's term, fraternal rather than pure conquest. And it can be more. It can also be a religious gesture. For

---

[22] Bovis, "Le sens catholique du travail et de la civilisation," pp. 359-61.

in the final accounting Christian thought sees more in labor than the natural satisfaction of a human instinct. It is not just a vital necessity but also a moral duty grounded upon the command-ment of God; sanctioned by the example of Christ, onetime a carpenter; and tirelessly reaffirmed by the Church which claims to be His bride and the society of His faithful. But since God never commands the unreasonable, theologians hold that work would not be a duty were it not true that through it we share in values to which we should otherwise remain strangers.

One of the first of these values to be recognized was the asceticomoral which even modern eschatologists are willing to praise. The fourth-century monks in the Egyptian desert appre-ciated, of course, the economic and social functions of work. Martha is necessary to Mary, Abbot Silvanus of Sinai told a visitor who would not interrupt his prayer to join in the commu-nity labor. At harvest time, moreover, the monks often hired themselves out to earn grain, not only for their own needs but also for the Alexandrian poor. Yet even if circumstances dimin-ished the pressure of economic necessity, work was still valued as an ascetical discipline. The classical illustration is that of St. Paul the Hermit, who, deep in the desert and too far from any market where he might peddle his wares, adequately sup-plied anyhow with food from the date palms and his little gar-den, still spent part of each day weaving baskets. He knew the advantages of such employment, says Cassian, "for the sole purging of the heart, the steadying of thought, perseverance in the cell, and the conquest and final overthrow of accidie it-self."[23] Many others have learned the same lesson and found for themselves that work is often the way out of those moods of depression which paralyze the spirit.

---

[23] From Cassian's conference, "Of Accidie," in Helen Waddell, translator, *The Desert Fathers*, p. 232 (London: Constable and Company, 1936). For the com-ment of Silvanus see this same admirable volume, p. 198.

Today, although this ascetical function of work is by no means denied, it does share consideration with another religious finality of labor. The phrases which sum this up have become almost conventional in the context. For a sacramental character is said to accrue to work insofar as it constitutes a "collaboration" or "cooperation" with God for both natural and supernatural goals in the life of the individual and in the life of the community. Labor has its distinctive part to play as men move toward the supernal goal of divine union, for by the disposition of Providence it is one of the modes whereby the human creature shares in the work of creation itself.

Shares in the first place in the work of natural creation, in the unfolding of this world of inanimate elements, of vegetable, brute, and human life. The world as God has committed it to us was, so to speak, largely unformed and the Creator has unfolded it by working in and through the hands and intelligences of men who in their labor imitate, after a faint fashion, God's creative splendor and thereby manifest the special divine signature placed upon them. It is true that curious ambiguities and enormous abuses have obscured this vision across the centuries and have deflected men from its reasonable pursuit. But neither the Greek disparagement nor modern exaggerations of technical enterprise invalidate this concept of work as the collaboration of a free instrument in the continuing task of creation. The Church, said Leo XIII, "never objects to search being made for things that minister to the refinements and comforts of life." On the contrary, she condemns sloth and "earnestly wishes that the talents of men may bear more and more abundant fruit by cultivation and exercise." Thus she encourages genuine progress and seeks only to make sure that human industry does not divert men from God rather than conduct them to Him.[24]

---

[24] Leo XIII, "On the Christian Constitution of States," in Gilson, *The Church Speaks to the Modern World,* p. 179.

Christian thinkers have also recognized the potentiality of work for the education of character even at the natural level. They observe how laboring men become conscious of themselves, their freedom, and their limitation and how they manifest in work their divine likeness by exercising and intensifying the coefficients of intelligence and liberty, those powers which constitute man not merely the *vestigium* but the *imago Dei*.

Often enough, too, our natural abilities and tastes incline us toward a particular occupation, and some theologians remark that we may see in this an indication of the Divine Wisdom helping us map out an important area of life. Catholic writers will not push this theme as far as Luther did, since they reserve *vocation* in the strict sense for callings more comprehensive than a trade or profession: consecration to God in religion, marriage, and a dedicated life of celibacy in the world. But the vocation, for instance, of the husband and father includes within its full scope his occupation. On the other hand, the notion that a man's farming or business or profession is the central sacred reality of his existence leads logically to the Puritan industrialist who lives only to work. Catholic writers are prepared, however, to see in the convergence of aptitude and preference an *avocation*, a sign pointing to the work in which a man will probably best serve God and achieve himself.[25] In this sense the métier answers to an interior call without imposing the obligations of a total or irreversible career.

In such ways does Christianity illumine work even as a natural phenomenon. Had Adam never sinned or had humanity never been summoned to a supernatural destiny, work would still have been this duty of divine collaboration. The actual course of human history, however, marked by the fall and the

---

[25] Jose Todoli, "The Theology of Work," *Theology Digest* 2:176, Autumn 1954. See also H. Rondet, "Eléments pour une théologie du travail," *Nouvelle Revue Théologique* 77:30, January 1955.

atonement, reveals in labor a final and most noble dimension. For as the dogma of creation inspires Christians to work at developing material and human virtualities, so the dogma of the incarnation summons them to cooperate through their labor, among other ways, in the redemption of the world and time. This idea is not, of course, entirely acceptable to eschatological theologians, especially the Protestant ones. Among Catholics, however, the incarnational theme is often effectively voiced. We are reminded that, while the transcendent destiny of the individual is to realize in himself the fruit of the redemption objectively wrought by the Word, still the total Christian task extends further and its aim is to impregnate all things human with the spirit of the Lord. In other words, just as work expands the natural dimensions of the individual personality and the human community, so too it contributes to the unfolding of supernatural creation although the mode of influence is not, of course, the same in both cases.

In the supernatural order work does not play the role of a cause as it does on the natural plane. It operates rather as an extrinsic condition which expedites the achievement of the supernatural values. It can, for example, remove certain moral and physical obstacles to grace. The personality of the idler is no favorable terrain for the expansion of grace's action. Were he to develop the equilibrium which habits of work confer this divine action could be deployed more fruitfully, for grace builds on nature.[26] On the positive side, their work will confront men with numerous chances for those significant choices between good and evil which critically shape character. A great deal of work, thus far at least in human history, is streaked with boredom and strain and tempts us to laziness or selfishness. On the other hand, the very rewards of work solicit us to overabsorption in our occupations and to violent struggle for riches and prefer-

---

[26] Bovis, "Le sens catholique du travail et de la civilisation," pp. 369, 477.

ments. Thus the moment of work becomes, says Bovis, a time of option and of grace accepted or refused. Work will often demand that we prove our fidelity to our professional conscience and show ourselves seriously responsible and charitable. It will serve, besides, as a healthy astringent subduing egotism by letting us discover how puny our individual contribution really is. Thus work provides at least the occasion for supernatural growth because it presents a man with progressively more difficult and more noble value choices.[27] It was this truth which evaded Irving Babbitt, for he did not realize that the ethical exertions he prized so highly are, more often than not, closely interwoven with the whole life-sustaining labor of ordinary men.

That labor also has a sort of supernatural social value. For work, as we have noted often before, is a principle of community, and such fraternal communion itself prepares and purifies the natural base for supernatural community among men. Whenever society is rendered more humane by work, whenever their labor provides men with enough margin for the pursuit of virtue, whenever it promotes mutual cooperation, it helps to redeem human institutions and render them more perfectly instrumental for higher ends. Moreover, work ought to be, as Eric Gill said, "evangelical." That is, the Christian worker should provide his neighbors with the inspiration of good example even as he should share with them the fruits of his toil.

Man's supreme vocation, says Christianity, is to become through grace what Christ is by nature: a son of God. The fathers put this into bold formulae. Only of Christ, wrote St. Cyril of Jerusalem, does God say: "This *is* My Son." For He was ever the Son. Still, once the Holy Spirit has descended upon us, the paternal voice from on high affirms: "This man has now become My son." And St. Basil, describing the effects of habitual grace, concludes: "Hence it is that you become divine." Now, a

---

[27] *Ibid.*, p. 369.

great deal of the Christian view of work can be summed up in Mounier's explosive sentence applying this doctrine of divine adoption to the problem at hand. "If man is made to become god, whether naturally or supernaturally, he cannot accept that his wisdom should lie in a prudent and monotonous conformity to a nature once and for all defined. . . . Man . . . is essentially *artifex*."[28]

THE CONCRETE SITUATION OF WORK

These discussions which focus on the ideal nature of work may strike those who know the real conditions of much of the world's labor as excessively lyrical. And it would indeed be naive to think that the personal and social values of work can be fully realized without first undertaking a terrifyingly complex process of purification. As a matter of fact, most of the papal and episcopal pronouncements and most of the intellectual effort expended by Catholics on the problem of work during the past century have been concerned with the abuses depersonalizing labor. For although the problem is intrinsically spiritual, its solution must involve a good deal of juridical and politico-economic thinking. Consequently there has been a concentration on such questions as the social and legal character of labor; the right to a living wage, to property, and to free unionization; the labor contract and capital.

In all these sectors the problems have been very real even though some of them are less pressing now than they once were. At the moment of writing *Rerum novarum* Leo XIII declared that "working men have been surrendered, isolated and helpless, to the hard-heartedness of employers and the greed of unchecked competition." Concentration of economic resources in the hands of the few, he continued, meant that the wealthy mi-

---

[28] Emmanuel Mounier, *Be Not Afraid: Studies in Personalist Sociology*, translated by Cynthia Rowland, p. 18. New York: Harper and Brothers, 1954.

nority laid upon the laboring poor a yoke little better than that
of slavery itself. Forty years later Pius XI could still sum up
the whole economic order as one "hard, cruel and relentless" in
which the ambition for power had succeeded the desire for gain.
And in a famous, haunting sentence he pointed up the distortion
which has so often accompanied the expansion of machine industrialism: "So bodily labor, which was decreed by Providence
for the good of man's body and soul, even after original sin, has
everywhere been changed into an instrument of strange perversion: for dead matter leaves the factory ennobled and transformed, where men are corrupted and degraded."[29] Should
Americans feel that this is rather strong and hardly a description of their own industrial conditions—though it is by no
means certain that these phrases are inapplicable to us—they
must remember that the vision of the popes embraces the whole
world, and life in the steel mills of Anshan or the African mines
or communist farming communes may be light-years distant
from the atmosphere of the best American plants.

Despite all the real abuses, however, the most representative
Catholic thought has never held that such defects are fundamentally inseparable from machinism or the western economic
system. Writing in *Quadragesimo anno* of his predecessor's
work, Pius XI said: "Leo XIII's whole endeavor was to adjust
the economic regime to the standards of true order; whence it
follows that the system itself is not to be condemned. And surely
it is not vicious of its very nature."[30] Thus, here as everywhere,
authentic Christian thought holds to a central position between
the extravagant confidence of a laissez-faire economics and the
equally extravagant denunciations of the Marxists. From the
multitude of problems clustering about the actual situation of
work, however, two representative issues may be singled out

---

[29] Pius XI, *Reconstructing the Social Order*, pp. 28, 36.
[30] *Ibid.*, p. 27.

now: the modern problem of the machine and the perennial problem of pain in work.

Broadly speaking, the debate over the machine divides the contestants into three camps. At one extreme are the headlong enthusiasts who defend machinism without qualification. They are often seized by that technological spirit which Pius XII denounced because it makes technology the supreme form of human activity. The French sometimes call this *Fordisme;* and if one wishes to fob it off on the Soviets, one will speak of Stakhanovism. In any case, it is real and dangerous enough to become the easy target of another extreme wing which enrolls certain scientists along with some theologians, philosophers, and men of letters. This group regards all technical efforts as insignificant gestures, hardly worth attention in the long view, and it dismisses the machine as only the unloveliest item in the whole gruesome picture.

The most formidable and articulate opponents of modern mechanization are, however, the philosophers and artists who occupy the middle ground. As Mounier noted, these critics are not opposed to technology itself but only to machinism, which they believe destructive of craftsmanship and its distinctive rewards. We have noticed Eric Gill as an outstanding spokesman for this viewpoint. He was firmly convinced that, unless large-scale mechanized industry was replaced by independent craftsmen—who, of course, could employ smaller machines—there was no hope of recapturing the dignity and values of work. To those who protested that clocks can't be turned back he retorted fiercely that, unless this one were, ruin awaited our age despite all its scientific and industrial conquests.

This point of view has its bitter force, but it is also susceptible of certain criticisms and has gotten them from another gifted Catholic layman, one whose life of service and sacrifice wrote a stirring page in the history of contemporary French life. Emmanuel Mounier was in his mid-forties when he died in 1950.

As a young philosopher he had given up his academic post to conduct the review *Esprit,* an organ of the personalist movement which hoped to assist in the task of social reconstruction. Mounier was by no means a bubbling Rotarian. His aim was economic and spiritual revolution and the peaceful replacement of imperfect political forms by better ones. As he saw it, the revolution must include a humanization of machine work rather than its rejection. The antimachinist mentality had, he believed, a variety of sources. Sometimes it was the product of a narrowly bookish education which induced a hatred of machine in people who had never touched one. Sometimes it was due to a faulty historical sense which judged machines in terms of the society that first employed them, as if to say that, since Manchester in the 1830's was deplorable, so is machinism itself. Mounier insisted on the distinction between misuse and native defect. It is likely, he thought, that, as men grow more accustomed to machines, they will handle them better and be able to "humanize the inhuman forces of paleo-machinism." He argued, as others have, that the products of machine facture have a beauty all their own and that industrial life provides a good apprenticeship to the discipline of responsibility and the virtues of honesty and fraternal feeling. "Under the guidance of the human mind," he wrote, "technics only break with life in order to lead us from a condition of immanent servitude to an inhuman nature, to a considered mastery over a humanized nature."[31]

This may not seem much more realistic than the enthusiasms of the craftsmanship school, yet, all things considered, a reasonable optimism about the machine finds support in papal pronouncements and the reflections of Catholic theologians. These certainly deplore the abuses which have robbed work of its ra-

---

[31] Mounier, *Be Not Afraid,* p. 49. The substance of Mounier's critique is found in the section of this book to which the subtitle "The Case against the Machine" has been given, pp. 27-64.

tional character or promoted the fearful worship of technology which amounts to a materialism. But Pius XII could also write: "The people have welcomed, and rightly so, technological progress because it eases the burden of toil and increases production."[32] The era of technical civilization has secured men more firmly than ever before from the uncertainties of their natural environment; and this is itself, as some theologians observe, a kind of prophetic announcement of Christ's return, since it foreshadows the condition of the incorruptible city of God. It will be said that the machine age has also produced the hydrogen bomb. Yet Hiroshima is to be blamed, not on technology itself, but on the fatal human weakness which makes possible the perversion of all man's explorations and successes. In the very discourse which contained his severest indictment of technological excesses, Pius XII insisted that the achievements of industrial civilization could and should support a truly human life and assist its passage to fulfillment in the vision of God.

PAIN IN WORK

In his labor, said Adam Smith, a man must always lay down a portion of his ease, his liberty, and his happiness. At least, it is true that so far in history the element of hardness has not been excised from work. As a matter of fact, some depreciation of the worker and consequently some pain seem naturally inseparable from a good deal of human labor. No doubt there are occupations so interesting in themselves that the skilled worker is chiefly conscious of joy and satisfaction. But even in these cases, if the hours of work are unduly prolonged, the occupation is likely to become burdensome. Can it be hoped that these painful elements will be completely dissipated once society is so thoroughly purified that automation has erased toil, the workday is reasonable in length, shops and offices are pleasant as clubs, and

---

[32] Pius XII, "Christmas Eve Address: 1953," p. 178.

the work force has become a fraternal community? It does not seem likely. The creative pioneers will always extend themselves far beyond the limits of a forty-hour week and their achievement will be bought at a price. Moreover, some technological progress actually increases pressures. It is more taxing to drive a locomotive than an oxcart. But quite apart from these cases, there is reason to think that the source of pain in work can never be completely uprooted. "Work in itself," one theologian has written, "does not necessarily imply hardship. It includes hardship only in the sense that man is a being that encounters resistance in himself and in the objects on which he works."[33]

But this diagnosis suggests that the arduous character of work, the weariness and suffering that often accompany it, are rather natural. It was only in the state of paradisiacal innocence that the naturally deleterious effects of those resistances were gratuitously suspended by Divine Providence, leaving production sheerly joyous. In Eden, says St. Thomas, man would have worked *(operaretur)*, but his cultivation of the garden would not have been toilsome *(laboriosa)*. Now that those supernatural benefits have been lost, man's condition is no worse intrinsically than it would have been had he existed from the outset in a purely natural order. When we work, physical conditions inevitably operate and friction and usage make some inroads upon the organism. Work is abrasive even when every susceptible circumstance is controlled.

Nevertheless, as Pius XII has noted, the nobility and rights of that labor which masters the earth and enriches the personality are not diminished by the burden of fatigue associated with it in the present dispensation.[34] Moreover, Christianity's unique religious perspective makes it possible to enhance incomparably

---

[33] Todoli, "The Theology of Work," p. 176.
[34] Pius XII, "The Rights of Man" (Christmas Message, 1942), in G. D. Smith, translator, *Selected Letters and Addresses of Pius XII*, p. 291. London: Catholic Truth Society, 1949.

the present significance of the moment of work quite apart from its instrumental uses as a thrust toward the future.

This enhancement, in turn, does a great deal to strengthen the joy of work by counterbalancing that anguish which is due precisely to the way work subjects men to process and the relentless law of finality. The man who labors is always straining toward the future, and so long as a project is under way he is plunged into the stream of becoming. Whoever has worked intensely knows that preoccupation and anxiety about the outcome may soak up all thought; rob everything else of savor as all energies are bent toward the goal yet to be attained. Simone Weil was surely right when she said that "work makes us experience in the most exhausting manner the phenomenon of finality rebounding like a ball."[35] Now, if reality is entirely equated with becoming or if the only value in life is work-in-itself, men will be continually oriented toward the future. It is always the famous case of jam tomorrow but no jam today. From this viewpoint the only worth the present moment has lies in its instrumental function as it constructs the new world which is always arriving but never arrived.

In this climate, work ends by losing much of its native joy. The Christian genius, however, equilibrates the futurism inherent in all technical effort with several measures which do not negate the social and creative rewards of work but enlarge and complete them. For one thing, it inserts work into an ordered rank of values where its proper worth is acknowledged but not exaggerated. Its anthropology is also enlightening, for to understand the psychological tension natural to a being composed of matter and spirit is to understand why labor is always somewhat straightening. The goal can be visualized in a flash but it is reached only step by weary step. Above all, Christian insight

---

[35] Simone Weil, *Gravity and Grace*, translated by Arthur Wills, pp. 233-34. New York: G. P. Putnam's Sons, 1952.

tempers work's saturation in finality by drawing out, not only the intrinsic rewards of creative activity itself, but also its unique moral content. The moment of work appears now as one of ethical choice, capable of becoming the occasion of cooperation with the divine designs. In the act of working a man accepts, as we noted above, the demands of his human vocation and forges constantly his own character for good or ill. By his fidelity to this "sacrament of the present moment" the Christian finds a mode of divine union through effective charity.

But Christian thought can go even further. It can render intelligible the pain of work and unrewarding exertion; it can provide a recipe for transmuting these dolors into rewards of another coinage.

In the workaday world a great deal of labor is darkly smeared with toil. Perhaps even the scrubbing of latrines can afford some satisfaction in a job well done, but there are routine industrial jobs which seem totally devoid of the least spiritual recompense. Besides, the powerful ascendancy of economic and competitive pressures may snuff out what real possibilities of joy do exist. Yet even in such junctures the religious finality of work can still redeem the time and uncover a concurrent satisfaction in the accomplishment of the most arid task. For since Christianity knows how suffering may be utilized, it can show the man of faith a precious, ultimate value even in sheer drudgery emptied of all gratification. Working people, said Simone Weil again, need poetry more than bread. "They need that their life should be a poem. They need some light from eternity. Religion alone can be the source of such poetry."[36] When fatigue and monotony are consciously accepted because the workman wishes to attest his loyalty to God by loyalty to the human condition, these sufferings become actualizations of love. And the love is redemptive; for the discipline of fidelity, besides bracing

---

[36] *Ibid.*, p. 235.

the moral fiber, is itself a work of expiation. In this light no work is contemptible, since every occupation can sustain such a transmutation. At this level the work of the scrubwoman may be as powerful a gesture as the splitting of the atom or the speculation of a *Summa*. Here the sociologist's chart of prestige and nonprestige work has no place. The roughest labor may be clothed with the rarest distinction as homage to God writes itself in the offering of sweat and sorrow and as fraternal service emerges as the fruit of a true expenditure of self. Indeed, this courageous adherence to work despite its bruising impact can be, as Paul told the Colossians, a very special charity toward others, a cry to heaven on their behalf: "I rejoice now in the sufferings I bear for your sake."

WORK AND THE RHYTHM OF LIFE

> Reasonable rest and recreation [are] bound up essentially with the rhythm of an ordered life, in which rest and toil alternate in a single pattern and are integrated into a single harmony.[37]

It is axiomatic that nothing is fully understood so long as it is studied only in isolation. It also needs to be seen in its various relationships and in the role it plays when it is part of an organic whole. Consequently a final strand of the Christian theory of work needs to be picked out here. It is an obvious enough theme but one critically significant for life and education. For the Christian, rejecting all monisms, insists that work is but a single factor in human experience and is properly proportioned only if harmoniously integrated with moments of rest and contemplative reflection. Jean Lacroix has remarked that, were life synonymous with labor, men would not escape being themselves naturalized by their work at the very moment when they were humanizing nature. We may add that the potentialities of work

---

[37] Pius XII, "Christmas Eve Address: 1953."

itself are fully grasped only by men who come to it enlarged and enlightened by all the other distinctively human experiences of an integral life.

Such a life will include the dynamic exercise of reflective powers for an understanding of oneself and the universe. Without this meditation one would not recognize the self-revelation awakened by work experience.[38] There must be place, too, for the entire affective life with its countless radiations toward God as well as toward one's neighbor and the precious insights that come when perception is heightened by charity. The fully human existence must also enclose another region hard to label satisfactorily but of great value. It might be called the region of leisure or contemplation, yet both these terms have misleading redolences. It is, at any rate, the locale of that inquiring spirit which seeks and savors wisdom for its own sake without practical reference to immediate problems. It is equally the realm of the artist or scientist and of the mother brooding over her sleeping child, her thoughtful mood suffused with affectivity. Philosophers frequent the lofty heights in this country, but the ordinary man knows its more modest elevations when he is stirred by a profound idea or some natural splendor or when he seizes for himself a universalized truth out of its vivid concrete particularization. What one writer calls the religious employment of leisure is found here, too. Not that prayer and familiarity with God are confined only to certain hours. On the contrary, they should penetrate everywhere. But one of the deepest meanings of the Sunday rest is found in its provision of a leisure in which the worker can gather his forces together and renew the consecration of his labor to God.

Such consecration is necessary if the best values of work are to be won. Lorenzo de' Medici once remarked that only men of noble birth could attain perfection. The poor who work with

---

[38] Lacroix, "La notion de travail," p. 18.

their hands and have no time to cultivate their minds are, he said, incapable of it.[39] And despite its obvious seignioral bias this opinion has a certain underlying realism, for like most men, the Magnifico knew that a fully satisfying life cannot consist of work alone but must compound several elements. He neither knew nor cared how the wage earners of fifteenth-century Florence were to achieve this blend, but his brutal appraisal of their condition had some point. For so long as their days held nothing but toil, they would inevitably be somewhat stunted. One need not entertain Lorenzo's gnostic notion of perfection to see that, if work acquires a totalitarian ascendancy, it not only diminishes the significance of life but itself becomes unintelligible. The practical problem of a work humanism is, in fact, one of synthesis. Rest and recreation, reflection and worship—those who have best understood the Christian life have always prescribed a proper dosage of each. "Come apart," said our Lord to His apostles, "and rest awhile." What is sought is the rhythm in a unified life of work and leisure, action and contemplation. One is not the other but one complements the other. David Riesman once remarked that the Catholic genius does not confuse labor with play or demand that work be "fun." But neither does it display the opposite tendency to devaluate one in favor of another or to draw such sharp distinctions that technical culture cannot be easily integrated with the total pattern of a broader fabric. It seeks, instead, to educate for a total and multizoned life which esteems the values of work but reaches also to areas and aims beyond those of technology.

Men differ mightily when they set out to define those aims and explore those areas. But whether they deny or defend the intrinsic good of labor, they will all agree that it is certainly

---

[39] See G. Renard and G. Weulersse, *Life and Work in Modern Europe: Fifteenth to Eighteenth Centuries,* translated by Margaret Richards, p. 16. New York: Alfred A. Knopf, 1926.

instrumental. For this reason it cannot possibly be understood in isolation, for the meaning of any tool is grasped only when it is seen in relation to its goal. And just as work cannot be comprehended if totally abstracted, so neither can its distinctive goodness be laid hold of unless labor is vitally amalgamated with those other human expressions which it companions and serves. For it is in virtue of these associations that the potentialities of work are actualized. All work, says Père Charmot, is the image of the workman. If a man brings to his labor a noble and rich spirit, then the most material task becomes a splendid enterprise. If he brings to his work a mean spirit, a savage mentality, then any labor will cease to be civilized.[40]

When there is place in life for all the arts, the aesthetic satisfactions of technics come into their own. When there is leisure, there is a chance to develop the intellectual maturity capable of insight into the deepest implications of human labor. When the base of society is a genuine communion in spiritual aspirations, the fraternization of men at work can expand into a true and rational brotherhood. Above all, where there is religious faith, men understand work's most noble finality. They understand it to be a collaboration with God Himself.

---

[40] F. Charmot, *L'humanisme et l'humain*, p. 178. Paris: Editions Spes, 1934.

Toward a Christian Humanism
of Work*

To define the relationship between work and education we must first understand the role of work in the ideally integral human life. Should it be the master there, or one of several partners, or only a slave in the cellar? The modern Promethean will answer by exalting labor and technological methods, while the modern Platonist will reduce them to the status of sheer tools important only as the support of leisure. Yet history and the testimony of the human consciousness suggest that each of these positions, though sound in the values it affirms, is weak in the exclusive character of these affirmations. Reflection convinces most of us that work is indeed a valuable ingredient but not the whole of human experience. And in the concrete order, as economic historians have pointed out, the problem of work has been most satisfactorily resolved by those cultures which arrive at a fairly happy synthesis of labor and life. Among the primitive peoples this balance was probably won by indistinction, so that the areas of work, play, and art easily melted into one another while the religious inspiration pervaded them all. Work was a community enterprise coordinated to the beat of chants and drums. Art and technics flowered together from the same soil

---

* Life . . . is always a synthesis—Pius XII.

while prayer and sacrifices brooded over their growth. Modern students of Haiti and the Virgin Islands report something similar. The workers there take their time and follow their inclinations. Holidays are frequent and industry unrolls against a backdrop of song, conversation, and joviality. The shattering exploits of modern technology have been accomplished, it is true, by people more work-conscious and more addicted to strict timetables than these easygoing men of tropical climates. Yet even here, industrial engineers are discovering that productive peaks are actually raised when work and recreation equitably divide life and when labor itself is seasoned with rest or lightened by music.

No doubt that pleasant primitive commingling of work with other aspects of life declined when the rulers of the ancient world built their pyramids and ziggurats, their colosseums and arches. The peasant or slave was then hardly more than a machine producing the splendors of technical ingenuity for the pleasure of a few. In the twelfth and thirteenth centuries of the Christian era, however, some synthesis seems to have been again achieved. One must beware of romanticizing the medieval picture, but a careful student of the epoch can still sum up its temper thus: "For the men of the Middle Ages work was not servitude but a way of enfranchisement for the soul."[1] The guild system, for instance, enhanced the prestige of work by clarifying the honorable status both of master and apprentice, by curbing the extravagances of unrestrained competition, and by agreeably alternating workdays with holydays. Moreover, the guilds themselves were societies of artisans or merchants united for enterprises of devotion and charity as well as for control of their common craft. To cite another illustration of this

---

[1] Joan Evans, *Life in Mediaeval France*, p. 170 (London: Oxford University Press, 1925). Raymond Ruyer, "Métaphysique du travail," *Revue de Métaphysique et de Morale* 53:214, April 1948, calls the religious view of work the most precious element of medieval Christianity.

medieval blend of work and religious inspiration, the people of
Chartres helped to build their cathedral by making up volunteer
bands to haul the construction materials. "They admit no one
into their company," wrote Archbishop Hugh of Rouen in 1145,
"unless he has been to confession, has renounced enmities and
revenges, and has reconciled himself with his enemies. That
done, they elect a chief, under whose direction they conduct
their waggons in silence and humility."[2]

Although high generalizations are risky, it seems safe to say
that the modern expansion of technical power upset that fragile
synthesis even while it was erasing many of the sources of hardness and brutality in medieval life. There had always been, of
course, some work specialization, for the small town of the
Periclean age needed only one carpenter or cobbler. But this
was a far cry from the refined division of labor demanded by
the machine and from the intricate economic and social struc-
tures erected on this base. The historical picture is certainly
more complex than the communist indictment will allow. But
when Marx charged that the proletarians were alienated from
the products of their labor, it was the loss of a harmonious synthesis that he really deplored. The life of the worker had become one-dimensional. It had a zone of labor, indeed, but too
many other zones were closed off or highly restricted.

But if the ideal goal is a harmonization of many humanizing factors in which work is a valued member acquiring fullest
significance from its place in the hierarchy, then education must
also aim at this balance. It will be no real synthesis, for example, if labor is so subjected to the service of leisure that life is
thought to begin only when work is done. On the other hand,
what Charmot called the spirit of *primarism* is equally unsatisfactory—that is to say, the notion that working people require
only a superficial and hasty exposure to a little science, a little

---

[2] Evans, *Life in Mediaeval France*, p. 174.

literature, and then they "know enough." It is not surprising to find that Christian philosophers of education not only want to modify a narrow intellectualism but also believe in opening the riches of a popular humanism to all men and women and in encouraging them to continue their education throughout their adult lives. A healthy democracy, remarked the American Catholic bishops in the 1919 Program of Social Reconstruction, cannot tolerate a purely industrial or trade education for any of its citizens. At the same time they called for "substantially universal" vocational preparation. And this is but one of many instances which indicate that the authentic Christian spirit always seeks balance rather than extremes. A Christian education would fail conspicuously if it nowhere ministered to the correlation of those two emphases summed up under the rubrics *academic* and *vocational.* Such a challenge to education seems peculiarly acute today, for once more men have at hand the materials needed for a successful synthesis and the resources for a wise exploitation of both labor and leisure. Once again there may be a chance to establish the full concord of all human values, including that of work, and to do this without abandoning our present level of technological advance.

A dialogue among philosophers of work, such as that reviewed in these pages, suggests the full register of value to which life and education should respond. Each of the several theories has its distinctive intuitions, and Christianity, besides, completes them all with the nuclear concept of the synthesis itself. One must attend, for instance, to such twentieth-century proponents of the Platonic accent as Babbitt, Hutchins, and Adler, for they defend aspects of the total human experience which are neglected by naturalisms. They insist on both the meditative and the pragmatic function of intelligence. They assert the importance of order as well as of process; and the Chicagoans, at least, admit the importance not only of metaphysics but even of theology. Moreover, they define clearly the genuine notion of productive leisure which is neither work nor idleness. Occasionally one encounters in the popular press witty articles arguing that the machine has really not expanded leisure but only created free time which various civic and domestic duties then absorb. These complaints, however, are based to some extent upon a misunderstanding of the serious and creative character of true leisure itself. No doubt there should be some hours just for loafing, but our modern Platonists have argued very effectively that this sort of thing is by no means the *raison d'être* of leisure. They have also forcefully reminded us that life is not coterminous with labor or thought with pragmatic inquiry, that educational aims are not limited to an introduction to technical and scientific learning, and that education itself is not a matter for youth alone. Other writers have made the same points, of course, and perhaps in a more balanced fashion, but Babbitt, Hutchins, and Adler attracted attention just because they did light the themes up with rhetorical skyrockets.

On the other hand, they do diminish the effectiveness of their case by salting it with polemics or formulating arguments in excessively rationalistic or voluntaristic terms. It is easy enough, besides, for readers to conclude that Babbitt's educational ideals are too aristocratic and almost entirely mediated through literary studies, while Hutchins and Adler have given their critics reason to believe that for them education means ranging about a vast library filled with canned ideas and principles. In theories of this sort general education is made to concern itself exclusively with the kind of intellectual, physical, and aesthetic culture which is considered the suitable enrichment of leisure. Education for work is reduced to direct vocational preparation on the job or in technical institutes after liberal schooling is finished. But this theory of education leaves untouched the question of work's own liberal function and does not consider the problem of integrating technology with other aspects of human culture.

At best, therefore, the insight of traditional humanism is only part of the picture. It needs to be enlarged by the Promethean accent, for this, too, is a deeply human insight. Most men are persuaded that reality may be approached along several different avenues, depending upon whether or not the prevailing spirit is speculative, affective, or practical. The positive valence of Marxism and instrumentalistic naturalism lies in their appreciation of the power of pragmatic intelligence, whose prime manifestation is found precisely in work. For in drawing out the multiple virtualities of wood, metals, power resources, and the fertile earth men do enter into the secrets of being. The engineer, the mechanic, the cook, and the farmer through their work actually penetrate deeply into the nature of reality and by discovering what matter can become they prove that they have read it more effectively than those who lack such skill and experience. "You work with this earth," said Pius XII some years ago to a gathering of Italian pottery makers, "to transform it from a dark and shapeless mass into something useful, beautiful and brilliant."[3] It is to the credit of your Promethean that he so clearly perceives and so firmly upholds this creative dignity of labor.

He knows, moreover, that work keeps us keenly aware of the processive nature of existence. No one who toils can entertain the notion that the real is immobile or change but a phantom. For he will have seen what a powerful motor labor is in this flowing universe where it humanizes infrahuman forces, actualizes many of our finest personal capacities, and builds the material base of our social life. On this point, at least, the communists often have a keener perception than ourselves. This was strikingly indicated in the late fall of 1957, when Dr. George F. Debetz, a distinguished Soviet anthropologist, came to the

---

[3] Pius XII, "Nobility of Work" (March 27, 1949), in Pollock, *The Mind of Pius XII*, p. 77.

United States as the first exchange scholar since the "cold war" began. He was asked in an interview whether scientists in his country feared excessive concentration on technology to the exclusion of the humanities. "I understand what you ask," Debetz replied. "But I don't see how such an idea can even come into your head. Progress is technology. If you like, that is the path toward liberty, equality and fraternity. Humanity must first free itself from the bonds of nature. Technology is the key to this freedom."[4] This was phrased with some exaggeration, perhaps, but the basic theme is sound. History itself is proof that men live progressively more rational lives as technical advance frees them from brute compulsion.

Again, it is not necessary to paint oneself into the corner of pragmatism in order to admit that work has a special significance for intellectual maturation insofar as it is a vital introduction to one method of inquiry, the method which laboratory science has refined. This benefit, which Dewey found so attractive, is certainly not to be scorned. In their daily work routine, men do encounter and successfully solve a good number of problems by testing practical hypotheses. The log does get the bushman across the stream and the efficient missile does confirm months of planning. This does not prove, though, that the instrumental attack is either the only or the most significant source of understanding. The very thinkers who profess exclusive allegiance to pragmatic method and referential ideas mix into their system theses derived by the quite different method of philosophic speculation. Their monistic epistemology is a deliverance of their metaphysical analyses, for it is quite beyond the range of science to prove that only its sort of inquiry is valid. Any naturalism, however, whether Marxism or not, inclines to dissolve tensions, not by distinction and synthesis, but by homogenizing the conflicting elements. In Marx's systematic for-

---

[4] *New York Times*, November 24, 1957.

mulation of his insight into the dignity of labor the theses on
the primacy of matter, on the equation of reality with process,
and on the ultimate economic determination of all civilization's
products are crucial. The apotheosis of work follows easily when
the empirical perception of its undeniable importance is enormously inflated by the injection of these propositions. Dewey, a
more subtle thinker, knew that technical activity actually claims
only a part of life's and the school's attention, and the label of
Prometheanism fits him less neatly. Nevertheless his philosophy
does delimit the vertical and horizontal reaches of human experience, so that his educational theory, like his ontology, shows
a certain reductionist tendency. If things are valuable simply
because they are desired and if all worthwhile knowledge is
patterned after the operational fruits of natural science, the universe turns rather gray. Its treasures are not really intrinsically
good; and even if they were, we could never know it. This is
one reason, perhaps, why Dewey's optimism seems rather joy-
less. The present never counts for very much with him, and his
aesthetics hardly make sufficient counterweight to the heavy list
of his metaphysics.

It is quite likely, however, that most of us would distrust the
intransigent restrictions of both these polar positions. We do
think that our work has more than exchange value, that our in-
teractions with the real world are more than instrumental, and
that our occupations, while often rewarding, do not exhaust the
possibilities either of life or of education. We are likely, then,
to favor a third approach to a humanism which will account for
work. This is that center way which calls for the integration into
a single unity of many values hierarchically ordered. It is prepared to exploit the distinctive goodness of human labor but at
the same time to fix its rank in a structure of ordered aims. The
Christian theory of work is just such a synthesis. It seeks to
avoid both the Platonic and the Promethean shoals while ratify-
ing the noblest aspirations of those stranded on either bank. If

work is for Marx the supreme good and for the literary humanists a pure means and for Dewey a means which is also as much
of an end as one can hope for, then the Christian ideal of synthesis may be said to think of work as an intermediate value
which is a goal in its own order yet related as an instrument to
aims of one higher. Consequently the recipe for an integral life
calls for a rhythm of labor and leisure and possession of the
characteristic benefits of each. It will be the basic task of education to mirror this rhythm in order to effect that splendid unity
of life and culture in which every truly human expression is an
organic part. An education of this sort cannot be sheerly charis-
matic nor sheerly secularistic, but must honor the total vocation
of man. This means, in the present case, that, if education is
going to develop man and if man is a worker, then education
must develop him as a worker. At the same time, if he is more
than a workman, his education will not be properly limited to
technical culture.

Both the Platonic and the Promethean accents, each in its
own way, reject the ideal of such a harmony between action and
contemplation. Each is influenced by the conviction that there
is, after all, some irreconcilable conflict between the traditional
concept of culture and work. They elect different methods of
resolving this tension but are agreed in suppressing or radically
downgrading one or other of the constituents. A Christian, on
the other hand, can appreciate whatever there is of value in
Marxian humanitarianism or the instrumentalist insight into
praxis or the Aristotelian analysis of fruitful meditation. But he
will feel, as Dewey would say, that the setting of these ideas is
not logically adequate. For he is persuaded that a full understanding of work is achieved only within the Christian framework even as historically the Judaeo-Christian morality, working
like a ferment in the historic process of western society has been
a powerful impulse in the quest for technological progress as a
foundation of social justice.

That Christian inspiration to fraternal charity, in fact, exerts some influence even after its dogmatic roots have been severed. Marx himself was raised in official Lutheranism and his humane ideals are certainly closer to the gospel themes elaborated by his schoolboy essays than they are to the spirit animating much of contemporary communism. It is impossible to read Dewey, either, without feeling that his social ideals also had Christian antecedents and that much of his thought aimed simply to supply these ideals with momentum derived from secular rather than religious considerations. It is worth noting that, of the writers studied in the preceding pages, only Babbitt, who had turned to Buddha and Aristotle for his spiritual outlook, had little to say about the dignity of manual labor.

The allure of this ideal of synthesis is, paradoxically enough, acknowledged by the very communists most enamored of Prometheanism. For despite the logical imperative of their system, not even the Marxists are willing in practice to define beatitude as a life devoted solely to labor. Marx himself relished the disparate pleasures of friendship, conversation, literature, and salty herring as well as those of work. Stalin saw quite plainly that the realization of the distinctive satisfactions of labor depends upon more than labor itself. What is wanted, he wrote in 1952, is a society so culturally advanced as to secure for all its members an "all-round development of their physical and mental abilities." To achieve this aim—phrased here conventionally enough for a college catalogue—he called for a workday of six or five hours which would allow plenty of free time, first for "all-round" education and thereafter for universal compulsory polytechnical training. Once this was done, he said, echoing Marx and Engels, work would have been converted into life's prime want, a pleasure instead of a burden.[5]

---

[5] J. Stalin, *Economic Problems of Socialism in the U.S.S.R.*, p. 76. Moscow: Foreign Languages Publishing House, 1952.

We argue here, however, that a truly successful partnership of those two factors, labor and leisure, is best realized within the perspective of Christianity. For the Christian world view, constructed as it is in the light both of faith and reason, gives a wonderfully full account of life in general and work in particular. Because it includes the religious dimension it not only reveals the loftiest finalities of work but also keeps technology duly subordinated and thereby preserves the deepest understanding of its instrumental functions. The Christian who has a genuine theological and philosophical perception of work's inherent goodness will not esteem it simply for its ascetical uses. At least, he ought not. It is perhaps true that some devout people have the uneasy feeling that to choose an occupation because it is satisfying or because it fits their aptitudes and interests is rather ignoble. Such a choice ought to be made, they imagine, only on the basis of some religious or service motive—and the more mortifying the work, the better. It is true, of course, that occupational choice ought not be so egocentric as to exclude or neglect work's religious and altruistic potentialities, but it is entirely wise to be guided by one's abilities and interests in these significant decisions. For these are themselves providential hints and drawings pointing to the avocation in which a man is likely best to attain ultimate fulfillment. Human wisdom itself recognizes how important it is for personal development and balanced living to find the occupation for which one is really well fitted, and that same Christian faith which best explains the burdens of labor is also ready to honor its joys.

It should be noted, finally, that the educational ideal of synthesis corresponds effortlessly to the portrait of man as himself the product of a synthesis of matter and spirit. Because Christianity recognizes this essentially composite character of human nature, it understands that life and culture must embody a similar composition. Man has a spiritual factor, and so the contemplative life is his. But his spirit is enfleshed, and so technical activity which joins the hand and the mind is equally connatural. Because intelligence operates both practically and speculatively, an ideal education will seek to develop something of both the artist and the philosopher in every person.

Of course, this conviction that the Christian world view best enhances the significance of work is not uncontested. Religious men may declare that technical progress leads logically to an affirmation of religious values; but their adversaries insist, on the contrary, that work disabuses men of faith in any Providence acting either in the social or natural order. It is true, to be sure, that as the farmer gathers in the harvest and as the welder watches the skyscraper rise they may marvel simply at their own ingenuity. Yet even those who think that work militates against religious belief extol labor for values which were either first clearly recognized in Christian cultures or at least found in Christianity their richest context. Work will be praised, for instance, because it renders nature more rational through the insertion of ideas or because it is a school of human solidarity. But Christianity is precisely that faith which most fully honors the ontological goodness of nature and the technological vocation of humanity, even as it is Christianity which preaches the double solidarity, natural and supernatural, of all men in Christ. One does not need to be a believer to see, at least, that Christianity provides a spacious setting for the effort to steer a middle path between labor-as-an-absolute and labor-as-a-sheer-tool and to arrive at a balanced humanism of work.

WORK AND EDUCATION

Every education involves some sort of occupational preparation. Even the aristocratic program outlined by Locke in his *Thoughts* was intended as a kind of professional training. It marked out a way of breeding for a gentleman's son because Locke considered the life of the English gentry a serious career in itself. Newman balanced his celebrated defense of liberal culture as a "good-in-itself" with an exposition of its concomitant utility. But this general sort of vocationalism is not at all the same thing as a genuine humanism of work aiming at some fusion of intellectual and technical culture in education as a preparation for their blend in adult life. It will not be easy to translate this ideal into the workable terms of a practical program, but its components are not intrinsically contradictory. The conflict between technics and other cultural expressions is neither natural nor inevitable. It has been historically real enough; and perhaps it will never be possible to balance the elements of manual arts and the traditional "humanities" in such a way that everyone is quite satisfied and the equilibrium itself solidly grounded. But theoretically the opposition is less real than apparent. St. Jerome is the very archetype of the early Christian humanist, the man who could not stop writing like Cicero even if he tried. And Jerome, outlining a little girl's education, spoke like a rhetorician when he advised: "Let her learn by heart so many verses in the Greek, but let her be instructed in the Latin [Scriptures] also." But he spoke rather differently when he added: "Let her learn too how to spin wool, to hold the distaff, to put the basket in her lap, to turn the spinning wheel and to shape the yarn with her thumb."[6] Doubtless the child's mother was familiar enough with all these details which Jerome counts out so importantly, but the picture of the quarrelsome old scholar carefully setting them down is certainly an instructive one.

A Christian humanism, then, must include among its general aims this particular one of a humanism of work. That, in turn, will have two complementary moments: education *for* work and education *through* work. These two phases, the reflec-

---

[6] St. Jerome, "Letter to Laeta," in Robert Ulich, editor, *Three Thousand Years of Educational Wisdom*, second edition, pp. 167-68. Cambridge: Harvard University Press, 1954.

tive and the operational, the theoretical and the practical, are related and proceed together, but the method of the one is not quite the method of the other. Education *for* work has two objectives of its own. It aims to equip young people with some religious and ethical appreciation of the nature and dignity of labor as well as with some recognition of the challenge imposed by the ambiguities enveloping many occupations in the contemporary world. If these distortions are due to socioeconomic defects or to an intellectual climate which pushes men into extreme positions, it will at least be salutary to know as much. Second, education for work ought to aim at helping young people make wise vocational choices and prepare them to understand and sustain the pressures of work life. Education *through* work, on the other hand, seeks to provide some practical experience of the distinctive intellectual and moral satisfactions of technological activity pursued for its educational potential rather than for gain.

To work these objectives out in any detail is, of course, a knotty problem. There is always the danger of forgetting that any viable program must have its feet on the ground. Schemes which are original but unreasonable are self-defeating, for they cannot win the assent of informed people. Every teacher has a bleak enough perception of school realities and can only regard as maddeningly fanciful the more rhapsodic interludes of pedagogical writings. The theorist needs to temper his canvas prudently and remember the drab facts: crowded classrooms, overloaded schedules, and the jolly profusion of report cards, admission slips, attendance records, and questionnaires; the students who are tired or sullen or bored and the teachers who are harried or mediocre; the lesson plans which looked so promising on paper and fell so flat; the faulty thermostat and the broken window shade. Of course, there are also shining hours and real if modest triumphs, but philosophers of education are less likely to ignore these than they are to overlook the concrete demands of the workaday world.

During the early years of the Great Depression, for instance, one writer suggested that to recover work's educational significance American industry should be slowed down to the point where it could employ half the people half the time, children included, without the danger of overproduction. While one can admire the generous idealism of the author, his recommendation was impractical and apt to make hardheaded people scornful. For there is little reason to believe that a humanism of work would really be expedited by returning children, even under purified conditions, to those industries from which years of struggle against child labor have partially rescued them. And in any event, it is amply clear that the dynamism of American industry carries it in the direction of increased power and speed, so that, while our political society retains its present basic features, the slowdown proposed is highly unlikely. Even in the depression years the trouble was not overproduction—plenty of people lacked even necessities—but rather that real wages had not kept pace with the increase in production and workers could not purchase the durable goods they were manufacturing. An educational theory of work must not, then, seek originality at the expense of realism. It is easier, of course, to provide a radical manifesto than it is to plan what Mounier called "the patient transformation of everyday life." But the manifesto is not likely to do justice to the complexities of either the existential situation or the speculative problem itself.

THREE THESES

The outline of a Christian humanism of work may be indicated in three interlocking theses which recapitulate many of our earlier observations. The first enunciates a global and basic aim. An adequate education for work must consciously envision a total life with its rhythm of labor and leisure unified by a religious outlook which penetrates and ultimately explains the highest function of both. The principles of this synthesis must be taught explicitly, for as Christopher Dawson once remarked, "It is not enough to put the Gospel by the side of modern technology and to leave the student to work out their relations with one another."[7] Then, in the second place, it should be observed that this humanism of work calls for a division of responsibility. It ought to be the cooperative enterprise of several agencies and must proceed on different planes. For part of the task the family is especially well qualified, while other aspects are more easily left to the concern of the school. Finally, it may be suggested that the common school will itself approach work in two ways as it provides some understanding and some concrete experience of work's potential.

The first thesis hardly needs much attention, since the ideal of synthesis has already been emphasized. Unless life is more than work, work itself cannot be properly human; and unless education's grasp reaches beyond technics, it cannot really train for work. All this is but a corollary from the instrumental character of labor, which attains intelligibility only within that serried order of values and purposes which it serves but does not determine. Concrete cases can be cited to show that work is fully appreciated only when related to the unified life of man within a context wider than the economic one itself. Everyone agrees that work can be, for example, a school of solidarity. But why is this so? Or to put it another way, why does it not seem to be so in many factories and offices? The simple fact that men are working together is not enough, it would appear, to snuff out the sparks of jealousy and ambition. One investigator recounts a rather typical incident in which an electrician warned his helper against sharing information with other workers in the shop. "When you help him he gets credit for what we know. If you don't help him he will have to go to the foreman for

---

[7] Christopher Dawson, Letter on "Christian Culture." *Commonweal* 61:678, April 1, 1955.

the information and then the foreman can tell who his good men are."[8]

Labor will nourish fraternity but it does not actually create the roots of true community. These are grounded in the human spirit, which makes it possible for men not only to conceive technical schemes and cherish noble hopes but also to share these with one another. If the inmates of a prison camp entertain common ideals of freedom and brotherhood, their enforced toil may indeed draw them together into community. If they do not, it will only provoke wrangling and betrayals. To see work as a school of solidarity, therefore, you must see more than work. You must see that the truths of justice, freedom, and fraternal love, abstract though their concepts may be, point to realities in which they are concretized. You must see, too, how men through their intelligence apprehend these values and through their self-determined choices incarnate them in their world.

Indeed, the materialist ought logically to be baffled by work, for it does involve the realization in matter of nonmaterial creative ideas. In his work a man grasps those potentialities of nature which nature itself cannot know, and his mind and heart conspire to draw into existence what was once but a dream of the spirit. The worker, therefore, transcends the conditions of the ponderable. He is its master, not its slave, and if he remembers this he will avoid the subtle temptation to subordinate his person to his product. For it is only too easy for men to commit themselves totally to their occupations when they see the power these deploy.

It is of prime importance, then, to develop technical culture and at the same time to relate it to all the other realms in which men live and act. Work has its precious contributions to make,

---

[8] S. B. Mathewson, *Restriction of Output among Unorganized Workers*, p. 27 (New York: Viking Press, 1931), quoted in Ross Stagner, *Psychology of Industrial Conflict*, p. 146 (New York: John Wiley and Sons, 1956).

but it is not the only educator of personality. As Mounier re-marked, it would be most dangerous to make it so. For in such a case those who found in labor the exclusive source of meaning and the sole pilot of character would be quite lost in their non-working hours and the increase of leisure would only intensify their distress.[9] Traditional schooling, however, has rarely been guilty of spending too much time on a humanistic interpretation of work. On the contrary, it could have made much more ex-plicit an understanding of technology in the light of history, aesthetics, metaphysics, and theology. Education always needs to point out in direct and coherent fashion how work becomes a medium for the aspirations of religion, fraternity, and creativ-ity. For these things are not learned by osmosis in the course of one's occupation nor through an occasional homily. That is clear enough if we consider the number of people who have worked hard all their lives without ever discovering therein anything more than an exchange value.

These lessons are taught, however, not by one but by many teachers, for those who learn them belong simultaneously to many communities and even from a purely practical standpoint it is clear that no single agency can fully induct students into all the phases of a humanism of work. The school, for example, is neither the home nor the church and cannot, even if it would, supply for the special influence which those societies bring to bear upon education. Some theorists, it is true, would try to meet this insufficiency of the school for the total task of educa-tion by creating a totalitarian political society which would sup-press or absorb all other communities. Man would then belong to but one vast public with all his life integrated under the cate-gory of citizenship. Whatever is to be taught about work would be taught by this society through its public institutions effec-tively controlling the entire schooling of the child. It would

---

[9] Mounier, *Be Not Afraid*, p. 54.

matter little whether this were the tyranny of a fascistic, communistic, or majoritarian dictatorship so long as the unique flower and form of the familial and religious societies were killed and freedom devoured by Leviathan. Such social monism might well be self-destructive in the long run. For it could triumph only by denying certain profound human longings and it is, consequently, suspect on empirical reckoning alone. Man's associative impulses cannot be satisfied by one monstrous political society without doing violence to the human person, for there are distinct values which nourish men and call for the family and the church as vessels of their conveyance.

If it be granted, then, that human existence unfolds within those three primary societies—the domestic, the religious, and the civic—as well as within many secondary groups, and if work is to be integrated with all of life, then the task of integration will very likely employ the characteristic energies of each of these chief societies. As a child moves from one of these spheres to another, he should at least find work everywhere honored. Moreover, the domestic and religious communities have explicit roles to play in educating for work. So, too, has the school, particularly when it is free to reflect the deepest religious idealism of a family or a people and consequently able to develop the theological dimension of work. It would be unfortunate were the distinctive contributions of any one of these agencies lost because the vision of its responsible elders had atrophied. In such a case children might be led to think mistakenly that the serious work phase of life has no important links with the home or with the church or with the local community. Work might then appear an enigmatic pursuit to which fathers go in the morning and from which they return at evening, while the real life of the family or neighborhood begins only when this harsh but necessary business is done.

Since work supports life and matures personality, it has both an economic and a humanistic function, and the school will be concerned chiefly with the latter. If it be objected that work minus the economic motivation is not really work, the point need not be controverted, for one may simply speak instead of work activity. In fulfilling its responsibility toward this work activity the classroom need not turn itself into a miniature "society" with its own work projects scaled to size. Doubtless, a school has societal features, but it is pure artifice to pretend that it can adequately mirror the communities in which the real work of the world goes on. Children know this quite well. They know that the total population is not homogenous, not made up of people all nine years old and just so high. They know that there is a great difference between the handicrafts at school and the work done in shops, factories, offices, and their own home. It is more reasonable, therefore, to say as Dewey did that the school's part in educating *through* work is best done when work experience is *re*-presented on an altogether different level than the economic. On that plane the characteristic notes of work activity can be accented and technical formation can be introduced precisely as human formation.

If this be the case, though, it will be necessary to look elsewhere for an arena in which children may acquire some direct experience of work's economic function. Marx would have had the monolithic political commune provide that opportunity. The American as well as the Christian genius turns instead to the family circle and thereafter to the neighborhood community in an open democracy. This solution is ill-defined and conventional enough so long as one persists in thinking of education only in terms of the formal training given at school. It must be recognized that the family is always a potent educative force, either for good or evil, and that parents are naturally capable of fruitful and systematic teaching. Nevertheless the task of educating for work is not an easy one. Doubtless it is true that modern city and suburban life offer children fewer opportunities for varied and significant work than did the farm and village not so long ago. Even though the "do-it-yourself" movement has made it possible for adults to rediscover the joys of craftsmanship, children do not find a parallel opportunity for creative work because the sewing machine and the turret lathe are too formidable and too valuable to be entrusted to young hands.

Yet the creative impulses are there and deserve to have new outlets for their satisfaction discovered. Toy manufacturers, at least, have been canny enough to see that, if parents are exercising their amateur talents for painting and plastering, cutting, and stitching, their children will be keen to imitate them. The toy shop, accordingly, displays all sorts of hobby kits for constructing miniature furniture, assembling model cars and clocks, fussing with small-scale cookery, house cleaning and car washing. All this suggests that ours is indeed a civilization of work and needs only to be properly purified and interpreted. The conscious educational enterprise of parents in this area has two phases. They can, for one thing, provide their children with some experience of craftsmanship by supplying the simple tools and understanding guidance required for projects which fuse the inspirations of work and play: building a serviceable bench, baking cookies, wiring a toy stage or doll house, making simple articles of clothing and accessories. Those who have worked up the pedagogical techniques in these matters point out that parents need to be patient with children during the project, for the child's interest span is not that of an adult. The older person should work beside the younger so that he may explain intelligibly the need and significance of each step in the process.[10] And although the parent will emphasize the right way of doing

---

[10] Jerome Count, *When Your Child Dislikes Work*, p. 20 (Pittsfield: Work Education Foundation, 1955). The author is one of several who point out that parents dissatisfied with their own occupations cannot hope to educate children to a humanistic relish for the values of labor. He is also the director of a work camp in which young people are provided with work experiences aimed at developing sound attitudes toward work itself.

things as distinguished from the careless, he should be willing to settle for something less than perfection lest all the joy of work be corroded by anxiety.

Economists of psychological bent would see in these activities quite a special value just because they do blur the line between work and play, for they think that it is the sharp division between these two which accustoms modern man to consider labor painful and exacting and to overlook its satisfactions. Nevertheless what distinguishes real work from hobbies is just that fact that it must be done even when it has none of the flavor of play and freedom. Perhaps children can be reasonably introduced to this austere aspect when parents devise an intelligent plan for sharing the necessary household work and, at the same time, guide their children toward an appreciation of the social and religious values served by this cooperative activity. No doubt, chores which last too long or are too hard or too boring are undesirable because they acquaint children too forcibly with the burdens of labor. But if the child has a rational portion of common tasks and is held to their faithful performance, he may be expected to acquire some insight into the law of work as well as into its rewards.

This insight will hardly expand effectively, however, unless parents help to make it explicit. There is no automatic connection between dull chores and growth in wisdom or virtue.[11] It is up to parents to make the rudimentary tasks as meaningful as can be, so that their humanistic possibilities are understood. This cannot be done by brisk exhortation. It cannot be done at all unless the parents themselves relish the dignity of labor and can find a consecrated joy and self-realization in their own occupations. Then they may hope to instill desirable attitudes, not

---

[11] See on this point the report of an interesting empirical study by Dale B. Harris, Kenneth E. Clark, Arnold M. Rose, and Frances Valasek, "The Relationship of Children's Home Duties to an Attitude of Responsibility," *Child Development* 25:29-33, March 1954.

by preaching but by living them. The practitioner and the theoretician are agreed on this point, and it is indeed a common-
sense intuition. Parents who are dissatisfied with their own jobs
and disinclined to look for any compensatory creative outlet in
hobbies or domestic arts cannot hope to inspire their children
with any enthusiasm for work. The father and mother, on the
other hand, who work alongside their children and share with
them the dream and understanding concretized in the task at
hand as well as a care for decent craftsmanship do a great deal
for these young people. For they are accustoming them to find
genuine satisfactions in the work that will be theirs in the future,
and this is no mean gift.

Parents can equip themselves for this task of developing a
work humanism in a variety of ways. In one locality, for instance, when several families discovered that children objected
to chores on the grounds that none of their companions had to do
them, the parents broke the circularity by enlisting the school's
cooperation. The universal homework assignment one week end
was to help in some household task, and this strategy helped to
dissolve the collective prejudice. As a solution it may have been
somewhat ambiguous, but as the symbol of a shared approach
to a common problem it was significant. For it might never have
been devised were not these Christian parents accustomed to
meet fortnightly to discuss just such problems in the light of
their religious convictions.[12] It has been found, too, that the
inspiration and pattern of domestic cooperation in work can be
enlarged for an analogous application in neighborhood projects.
There are many instances on record of young people working
skillfully and loyally on community undertakings for no recompense beyond the intrinsic personal and social gains. Church
groups, for example, have organized efforts of this sort and teen-

---

[12] Bob Senser and Wilma Senser, "The Christian Family Movement." *America*
87:308-10, June 21, 1952.

agers have built roads and schools, farmed large tracts, helped resettle displaced persons. A fruitful conjunction, therefore, of work and education can be effected within family and local groups where it will avoid alike the unwholesome aspects of factory production and the more dreadful pressures of totalitarian society.

There remains a peripheral point of interest. In his *De tradendis disciplinis* the sixteenth-century Spanish humanist Vives outlined a fairly typical Renaissance education. He made, however, an unusual recommendation when he required pupils to pause and consider the economic aspects of life before going on to final studies in history, philosophy, and law. The schools need not dispense the information, he said, but the students, already mature, should go out and search for it by observing craftsmen in shops and factories. Is there not a worthwhile hint here? It would certainly be helpful if we enlarged our understanding of vocational areas other than our own, for such knowledge widens the base of communion. If the people who were so exasperated by the miners' strikes during the thirties had had some inkling of what work in the coal pits is like, they might have thought and spoken differently. A few industries have actually experimented with informal education of this sort by opening plants for tours while normal operations are under way. The Jones and Laughlin steel mills in Aliquippa, Pennsylvania employed most of the workers in town, but what they did was mysterious to the rest of the people until the firm ran several weeks of guided tours. Thousands made the trips and were astonished by the skill displayed in this world of flame and steel. Practical lessons were learned. One woman remarked that from now on she would be more patient with her husband if he came home in a grumpy mood, for she could understand why he might.[13]

---

[13] C. B. Palmer, "Industry Sets Up 'Open House.'" *New York Times Magazine,* p. 14, December 19, 1954.

THE SCHOOL

> There is no place closer to man than a workshop, and the intelligence of a man is not only in his head, but in his fingers too.[14]

To see how technical culture fits into a scheme of general liberal education one must draw together various insights. For if Marx's sweeping philosophy of labor suggests that work life is entitled to academic representation, Dewey has indicated the precise formality under which it is to be represented and the traditional humanists keep us from forgetting that it is a matter of proportionate representation. It is not now a question of vocational institutes and professional schools whose purposes unfold after or apart from the period of general schooling. It is rather a question of the role to be played by work experience in the development, not of the specialist, but of the normally mature—the liberally educated—man or woman. For if the demands of craftsmanship challenge any workman to reflect, plan, choose, and endure, then they too are liberalizing, for they nurture the uniquely human powers of thought and free choice.

Our concern is with the education given at the elementary and the secondary levels. The problems that beset these schools today are certainly legion. On the one hand they have a real, though remote, vocational character even if they do not attempt direct job training. This vocational accent, however, is not the whole story, for these schools are also expected to cultivate intelligence and character as desirable goals in themselves. It is sometimes said that lower schools should initiate a process which flowers in the liberal-arts colleges and has as one of its distinctive products a love of wisdom for its own sake. Those who are interested in exploiting the sapiential resources of work also cherish this ideal. They argue, however, against oversharp

---

[14] Jacques Maritain, *Education at the Crossroads.* New Haven: Yale University Press, 1943.

division of the liberal from the technical, and they believe that one need not deny the instrumental uses of liberal education in order to relish its native goodness. In any event, the years of general education are expected to accomplish enormous tasks. They are supposed to leave young people with some awareness of the literary, scientific, philosophical, and religious forces in our traditional culture. Their perspective must be broad enough, too, to envision man's total career, which includes a constant responsibility before God, and its numerous particularizations in responsibility for oneself and for the common tasks of the human community.

All this makes, indeed, for a formidable academic program. For it is surely worthwhile if young people have mastered a foreign language, can read substantial books intelligently, and themselves speak and write with clarity and a dash of grace. It is desirable that they be introduced to science and mathematics lest real talent for these studies be lost forever through ignorance of their very existence. It is desirable, too, that they have begun to make factual appraisals of the contemporary scene in light of a knowledge of the past, to taste the delights of music and the plastic arts, not as spectators only, but as performers. It is supremely necessary that they have entered by thought and action more fully into their religious faith. We have already remarked that such a program as this requires plenty of that disciplined effort which is a general requisite of all serious work so that demanding studies themselves provide concrete experience of the law of labor.

But in view of this ambitious program we must grant that the school can allot to the humanism of work only a proportionate place. This will not even be the prime place, for the school today is the only agency of systematic intellectual culture and this is its specific task. It has, indeed, a guidance function; it includes programs of physical training. But these responsibilities do not fall to it exclusively and neither does it have sole care for development of a work humanism. Nevertheless it does have distinctive contributions to make to that humanism on the planes of both understanding and practice.

To begin with, the school has some concern for the students' selection of their future occupations, since it certainly has some influence on that choice. It was once commonly claimed that the liberal college prepared for life, not for making a living. Yet the curriculum of this college did condition occupational choice, since it was understood to be the usual prerequisite for certain professional and managerial careers from which those who had not gone through this course were effectively barred. In any event, the high school and college cannot ignore a question which its students are actually deciding during the years they spend in these schools. Such decisions are clearly crucial. A man's entire personal history and even his achievement of greater or less moral stature may depend to a considerable extent upon the character of his experience at work. It will make a great deal of difference whether he realizes therein some success and the satisfaction of feeling himself to contribute to the human heritage or whether he knows only boredom, frustration, and failure. Since the critical selection is often made in terms of the alternatives with which education has acquainted young people, the school has to do more than administer a few vocational-preference tests. Serious damage may result if schools not only fail to awaken students to the possibility of careers in science, technology, or the arts but actually render these careers forever beyond their reach because the academic program never acknowledges their existence. It is neither necessary nor possible for the high school to examine in detail all occupations. It should be possible, however, for it to instill an appreciation of work in its fullness and to suggest something of its enormous contemporary variety: the mechanical and fine arts, theoretical and applied science, the professions, business, and service occupations.

Such an education for work would ideally prepare for wise occupational choice by developing a philosophical and theological understanding of work itself. This wide view of technical enterprise might constitute a unit in long-established curricular divisions. In the secondary school, for instance, it could be inserted into the social sciences or religion classes. At the collegiate level it could find a point of departure in philosophy or theology. Since it is something of an interdisciplinary venture, the study of work might also be comfortably housed in a niche of its own. On the other hand, the idea of integration appears very logically when theology or philosophy are drawn into the problem of work or when the social studies are drawn upward to the point where wider vistas open. To be sure, a school disbarred by law or custom from developing the resources of religion could go only part of the way here.

This theoretical phase must also include some reflection on the current social questions touching labor. We know that there are still people who oppose the principles of free unionism, governmental safeguards against wide-open markets, more equitable distribution of the national income, and federal insistence upon worker insurance against the hazards of old age and unemployment. Yet these are measures which go a long way toward humanizing work for masses of people. A school will do a great deal if it helps young persons appreciate worthwhile social advance of this sort and prepares them to continue the work of social purification and progress.

This sort of education is doubtless rather glancing in the lower grades. It is struck off briefly in social studies and religion classes and reflected from the personal attitudes of the teacher. It is to the high school and college that one must look for a consistent and explicit treatment of those questions in history, sociology, ethics, and theology. This is a moment of theory which may be supplemented by firsthand observation of plants, farms, and offices as well as by readings and informed discussions. Not many novelties are needed, though, for this is also an emphasis which can be introduced into the existing academic regime without any sharp transformations.

The school's second contribution to a humanism of work lies in the area of practical, concrete experience. Somewhere in its program it should find place for education *through* work, for a savoring of the actual rewards of craftsmanship as an exercise of pragmatic intelligence and the source of special creative and social satisfactions. This would supplement the work education given by the family or compensate for its neglect. Its aim, as Dewey knew, is to exploit those cultural virtualities which industry in its mechanized stages is not easily prepared to do. Later on, the technical and professional schools can train marketable skills. But the shops and hobby clubs of our lower schools should have in view work simply as one moment and means of a child's intellectual and moral growth. It is not necessary, therefore, for these shops to match the equipment and procedures of contemporary industry. On the contrary, the specific pattern of technical culture can be better learned, perhaps, through making by hand products currently machine-produced. The detailed division of labor, so fruitful for mass output, is pointless when the workman's own development is the aim. In the school workshop, then, the students set their own goals and plan their own strategy so far as this is feasible. Then they carry the project faithfully through to completion as well and honestly as they can. Thus they will discover both the rewards and the price of this sort of work, this making of things *well*. In that discovery lies a humanistic benefit as young craftsmen learn, not only the character and possibilities of matter, but something also of their own human condition. They taste in their work the actuality both of its law and its joy.

Christian educators will not require work projects to carry so large a share of the task of character education as Dewey would commit to them. They will not make social situations and conflicts the actual generators of moral rules and values, nor will they explain social ethics in strictly pragmatic terms. At the same time, they know very well that there is a vast difference between the speculative grasp of the nature, norms, and content of the morally good life and that life actually possessed. Moral education has a necessary instructional moment, but it can no more stop there than building can stop at the drawing board. The moment of practice must follow if ethical principles are to be transmuted into living fonts of action and if behavior is to correspond with belief. Aristotle and St. Thomas did not agree with Plato that virtue could be taught in the strict sense of the word. In the geometry class, indeed, the student is "taught" when he is brought to see for himself that two parallel lines never meet in an Euclidean universe. When he understands as much, the specific work of the teacher is done, for the student is, in this respect, a "geometer." The teacher can also conduct the same pupil to a theoretical appreciation of the meaning, necessity, and beauty of truthfulness, but that does not insure his being honest. When speaking of moral training, therefore, St. Thomas did not use *docere* (to teach) but, making a significant change of verbs, remarked that the child should be accustomed, *assuescere*, to acting virtuously; should be taught, as it were, through the practice of personal action.[15] A great deal of such ethical action, however, is altruistic and is unfolded in interpersonal relationships. It is quite true, therefore, that work projects during or after school or school-sponsored in the community can offer splendid opportunities for young people to discover those values of fraternity, generosity, and cooperation which are elsewhere taught rather abstractly.

How realistic are all these observations? Well, at the elementary level some sort of home economics or craftsmanship class has long been common. It is not apparent that this inspira-

---

15 St. Thomas Aquinas, *Commentarium in libros ethicorum*, Lib. 2, lect. 1.

tion should be barred from the high school. If the precollege curriculum has no room for it as a regular course offering, it can at least find place as a carefully planned and administered extracurricular item. It is well known that the academic regimen of an English public school like Eton is far stiffer than that of an American high school. Nevertheless the so-called "drawing schools" and "schools of mechanics" hold an honored place at Eton. These are actually what we would call extracurricular and provide students with some chance for serious wood and machine work, for clay modeling and pottery making, for painting in oils and water colors.[16] Such a venture is difficult to plan and costly to sustain, but it is not impossible.

Moreover, liberal formation through technical formation need not be limited to the days of youthful schooling. Whenever adult-education centers announce programs of shopwork or auto mechanics or classes in painting and sculpture they are swamped with applications. Since adult education often deliberately aims to complement and compensate, those whose early training was largely bookish will be particularly anxious to try their hand literally in the making of useful and beautiful things. Those whose education was heretofore largely technical may prefer to turn now to literature and philosophy.

There are philosophies of education whose primary and nearly exclusive focus is society itself. Because of his profound concern for the worth of the individual, a Christian educator may be more inclined to put persons in the foreground and then to see society as their conscious creation and indispensable matrix. But either point of view issues logically in an esteem for that work which so powerfully educates intelligence and character even as it builds civilizations. Man's labor must, therefore, be reckoned with in any attempt to locate adequately the ideals of

---

[16] See, for instance, Bernard Fergusson, *Eton Portrait*, pp. 103-18 (London: John Miles, 1937).

education. In the history of western thought such attempts have often been influenced by a tradition which puts the highest human value in the operation of speculative intelligence and is apt to equate wisdom with virtue—the goods of the soul, Aristotle called them. The same theme is woven into the sacred books of the East: Krishna's advice to Arguna as they pause on the battlefield has mostly to do with the ascetical techniques which emancipate the spirit for the joy of contemplation. No matter how impatient it may make the pragmatist, this persuasion will not die. Humanists of every age breathe new life into it. After all, the ideal is appealing enough, for our own experience suggests that it has some warrant. Thoughtful men would not really be willing to return to twenty again unless they could bring back with them the little wisdom they have garnered during the intervening years. That modest harvest is too dear to surrender.

Christians may regard this Hellenic ideal sympathetically but it is not really theirs. For one thing, Christianity does not envision first of all either wisdom or virtue, but men in their ordination to God. Besides, the cleavages of this traditional humanism are too sharp and it has too little respect for that technology which expands creation even as it ministers to both wisdom and charity. In the school, as in life, the Christian teacher would blend work and fruition. He would awaken the personality to the religious and human benefits of labor as well as to its instructive austerity and limitations. He would awaken it to an effective sense of moral responsibility for the problems besetting work today as well as to a savoring of the joys of craftsmanship itself. But he would also help young people nobly balance the values of technical culture with all the other riches of action and contemplation in the living synthesis of their own persons. For this alone guarantees that "rhythm of an ordered life," as Pius XII called it in his Christmas Eve discourse of 1953, "in which rest and toil alternate in a single pattern and are integrated into a single harmony."

Although the study of human work from the viewpoints not only of economics but also of theology, philosophy, sociology, and psychology is comparatively recent, the literature is already very considerable and is added to constantly. The footnote references in the preceding pages have indicated the principal items bearing directly upon the topics discussed in the various chapters. This bibliographical note is designed to serve as a selective list of a few of the most helpful and characteristic contributions to the study of particular facets of the total subject. Many of these writings also include full bibliographies of the topics with which they are concerned.

A general historical background for all these inquiries is provided by the historians of science, economics, and technology. Outstanding here is the comprehensive *A History of Technology*, edited by Charles Singer, E. J. Holmyard, and A. R. Hall. The first of the five massive volumes included under this title appeared in 1954 and the fifth and final one, which carries the story down to the opening of the twentieth century, was published in 1958 (Oxford: Clarendon Press). The account of labor and technology in the cultures of the West is also set forth by several volumes in an older series, "The History of Civilization," under the general editorship of C. K. Ogden. These include: G. Renard, *Life and Work in Prehistoric Times*, translated by R. T. Clark (New York: Alfred A. Knopf, 1929); Gustave Glotz, *Ancient Greece at Work*, translated by M. R. Dobie (New York: Alfred A. Knopf, 1926); Paul Louis, *Ancient Rome at Work*, translated by E. B. F. Wareing (New York: Alfred A. Knopf, 1927); Prosper Boissonnade, *Life and Work in Medieval Europe*, translated by Eileen Power (New York: Alfred A. Knopf, 1927); and G. Renard and G. Weulersse, *Life and Work in Modern Europe: Fifteenth to Eighteenth Centuries*, translated by Margaret Richards (New York: Alfred A. Knopf, 1926). A. C. Crombie's

213

Augustine to Galileo: The History of Science, A.D. 400-1650 (London: Falcon Press, 1952) is important here for it corrects many misapprehensions about the medieval attitude toward and practice of science and technology.

The distinctive insights achieved by a sociological approach to the question of work are exemplified both in a general survey, Theodore Caplow, *The Sociology of Work* (Minneapolis: The University of Minnesota Press, 1954) and in a more specialized investigation, Eli Ginzberg and others, *Occupational Choice: An Approach to a General Theory* (New York: Columbia University Press, 1951). The application of psychological findings and techniques to work problems is demonstrated in Anne Roe, *The Psychology of Occupations* (New York: John Wiley and Sons, 1956) and Donald E. Super, *The Psychology of Careers: An Introduction to Vocational Development* (New York: Harper and Brothers, 1957). For an introduction to the subject of industrial and vocational education see John S. Brubacher, *A History of the Problems of Education,* Chapter 4, "Economic Influences on Education" and Chapter 9, "Curriculum," pp. 278-84 (New York: McGraw-Hill Book Company, 1947).

Neither the economic historians nor the behavioral scientists directly attack the speculative questions linked to the phenomenon of work. For an introduction to such questions there are two useful books. A stimulating attempt to outline the various historical ideologies of work was made by Adriano Tilgher, *Work: What It Has Meant to Men through the Ages,* translated by Dorothy Canfield Fisher (London: George G. Harrap and Company, 1931). Tilgher's generalizations must often be qualified, however, in light of the detailed historical studies cited above. The best single book for an opening up of the philosophical and religious perspectives is that of Etienne Borne and François Henry, *A Philosophy of Work,* translated by Francis Jackson (London: Sheed and Ward, 1938). This is not a technical study but it consciously draws upon history, philosophy, and theology for its reflections and consequently indicates effectively the full dimensions of a complete theory of work. Its authors were much indebted to an earlier book which is now rather difficult to obtain: Johannes Haessle, *Das Arbeitsethos der Kirche: Nach Thomas von Aquin und Leo XIII* (Freiburg im Breisgau: Herder, 1923). From a sizable number of books, dissertations, and articles in which continental, and particularly French authors have surveyed the philosophical questions relevant to work, a few representative examples may be cited. Yves Simon, *Trois leçons sur le travail* (Paris: Pierre Tequi, 1938) is an inquiry on the plane of metaphysics. A summary of Simon's thought will be found in his brief essay, "The Concept of Work," in Robert B. Heywood, editor, *The Works of the Mind* (Chicago: The University of Chicago Press, 1947). All the other pieces in this collection, which includes contributions from Robert M. Hutchins and Mortimer Adler, are also pertinent. Three perceptive essays, broadly philosophical in score are: Ferdinand Gonseth, "De l'humanisation de la technique," *Dialectica* 10:99-112, June 6, 1956; Jean Lacroix, "La notion de travail," *La Vie Intellectuelle* 20:4-31, June 1952; and Raymond Ruyer, "Métaphysique du travail," *Revue de Métaphysique et de Morale* 53:26-54, 190-215, January, April 1948. Paul Guitton's *Le travail attrayant: Essai historique précédé d'une analyse théorique de l'idée de travail* (Rennes: Imprimerie Provinciale de l'Ouest, 1935) is a doctrinal dissertation whose theme is similar to that of Tilgher. Finally, there is a philosophical study of extraordinary richness and erudition which appeared after the present book had gone to press: Hannah Arendt's *The Human Condition* (Chicago: The University of Chicago Press, 1958). This inquiry into three basic expressions of man's *vita activa* insists upon a distinction, so sharp as to be questionable, between *work* and *labor;* that is to say, between a higher, creative form of fabrication and a lower, toilsome one which is a sort of necessary evil. It is, however, hostile toward the spirit behind modern efforts to formulate a humanism of work and dismisses in a footnote such writers as Yves Simon, Jean Lacroix, and M. -D. Chenu as representatives of a "type of idealization . . . frequent in liberal or left-wing Catholic thought in France" (*ibid.*, p. 141, n. 5). In its own right, however, Miss Arendt's book is the most detailed and impressive contemporary restatement of the classic apotheosis of the *vita contemplativa*.

For the theology of work there are, first of all, some studies which fill in the historical background: Arthur T. Geoghegan, *The Attitude towards Labor in Early Christianity and Ancient Culture* (Washington: The Catholic University of America Press, 1945) and Sylvester Michael Killeen, *The Philosophy of Labor According to Thomas Aquinas*

(Washington: The Catholic University of America Press, 1939). Both of these provide useful bibliographies. The best brief introduction to the contemporary discussions on the theological meaning of history and man's technical achievements therein is that by L. Malevez, "Deux théologies catholiques de l'histoire," *Bijdragen* 10:225-40, 1949. On the theology of work itself two studies, both with bibliographical guides to other writings on the subject, are particularly useful: André de Bovis, "Le sens catholique du travail et de la civilisation," *Nouvelle Revue Théologique* 72:357-71, 468-78, April, May 1950 and H. Rondet, "Eléments pour une théologie de travail," *Nouvelle Revue Théologique* 77:27-48, 123-43, January, February 1955. From a good number of other contributions to this field the little book of M. -D. Chenu, *Pour une théologie du travail* (Paris: Editions du Seuil, 1955), deserves special mention. A compact review from a rather out-of-the-way source is P. de Letter, "Wanted: A Theology of Work," *Clergy Monthly* 20:93-103, April 1956. Protestant theologians have also given this matter considerable attention and a distinguished representative of this tradition is Robert Lowry Calhoun's *God and the Common Life* (New York: Charles Scribner's Sons, 1935). Finally, there are essays by Catholic philosophers who in their reflections take account also of the theological dimension of a theory of work: Eric Gill, *Last Essays, passim* (London: Jonathan Cape, 1942); Dietrich von Hildebrand, *The New Tower of Babel*, pp. 205-43 (New York: P. J. Kenedy and Sons, 1953); Jacques Maritain, *Freedom in the Modern World*, translated by Richard O'Sullivan, pp. 193-214 (New York: Charles Scribner's Sons, 1936); Emmanuel Mounier, *Be Not Afraid: Studies in Personalist Sociology*, translated by Cynthia Rowland, pp. 27-64 (New York: Harper and Brothers, 1954). With these might be put Josef Pieper's *Leisure, the Basis of Culture*, translated by Alexander Dru (New York: Pantheon Books, 1952) save for the fact that the glorification of leisure and contemplation in this brief book is somewhat at the expense of an appreciation of work.

From the vast library on Marxism several titles with special relevance for the precise questions of the Marxist philosophies of man and education deserve to be underscored. For an introduction to Marx's early philosophical writings H. P. Adams, *Karl Marx in His Earlier Writings* (London: George Allen and Unwin, 1940) is most useful as

Vernon Venable's *Human Nature: The Marxian View* (New York: Alfred A. Knopf, 1945) is for the Marxian anthropology. Two essays which consider the import for humanism of Marxist teachings are Robert S. Cohen's "On the Marxist Philosophy of Education," in *Modern Philosophies and Education*, The Fifty-fourth Yearbook of the National Society for the Study of Education, pp. 175-214 (Chicago: The University of Chicago Press, 1955) and James Collins' "Marxist and Secular Humanism," *Social Order* 3:207-32, May-June 1953. Both of these provide helpful bibliographical suggestions. For an overview of the Marxian ideology as seen from rather different angles there are, first of all, Sidney Hook's two books, *Towards the Understanding of Karl Marx* (New York: John Day Company, 1933) and *From Hegel to Marx* (New York: Reynal and Hitchcock, 1936) written from the standpoint of American instrumentalism and the fine, brief study of Père Joseph Vincent Ducattillon, "Communist and Catholic Doctrine," in François Mauriac and others, *Communism and Christians*, translated by J. F. Scanlan (Westminster: Newman Press, 1949). This symposium first appeared in the late 1930's and includes suggestive essays by Nicholas Berdyaev and Denis de Rougemont among others.

General bibliographical guides to the philosophy of John Dewey are *A Bibliography of John Dewey* which was prepared by Milton Halsey Thomas (New York: Columbia University Press, 1939) and the listing, brought closer to date, which is found in the reissue of Paul Arthur Schilpp, editor, *The Philosophy of John Dewey*, second edition (New York: Tudor Publishing Company, 1951). If one wishes to approach Dewey's thought with the help of commentators, there are two good ones—the first friendly, the second critical, *viz.*, Sidney Hook, *John Dewey: An Intellectual Portrait* (New York: John Day Company, 1939) and William Taft Feldman, *The Philosophy of John Dewey: A Critical Analysis* (Baltimore: The Johns Hopkins Press, 1934). Dewey's view of the problem of work and education can be gathered from the following places in his writings: *Democracy and Education*, pp. 228-42, 293-305 (New York: The Macmillan Company, 1916); *Experience and Nature*, pp. 121-38 (Chicago: Open Court Publishing Company, 1925); *Human Nature and Conduct*, pp. 142-44 (New York: Henry Holt and Company, 1922); *The School and Society*, revised edition, *passim* (Chicago: The University of Chicago Press, 1915); and "Learning To

Earn: The Place of a Vocational Education in a Comprehensive Scheme of Public Education," *School and Society* 5:331-34, March 24, 1917.

A handy tool for the study of Irving Babbitt's thought is provided by the topical index to his writings which has been appended to the posthumous collection of essays: Irving Babbitt, *Spanish Character*, edited by Frederick Manchester, Rachel Giese, and William F. Giese (Boston: Houghton Mifflin Company, 1940). Because Babbitt's books were, to use Paul Elmer More's term, "circular" in their manner and because it is the same characteristic body of opinion about which they all circulate any one of them is a good introduction to their author. The characteristic reflections on work and leisure are most easily found, however, in *Democracy and Leadership*, pp. 188-213 (Boston: Houghton Mifflin Company, 1924) and throughout *Literature and the American College* (Boston: Houghton Mifflin Company, 1908) although scattered comments may be gleaned from any of his books. From among the publications of Mortimer J. Adler and Robert M. Hutchins, the most pertinent for the topic of work's educational value would include Adler's essays, "Labor, Leisure, and Liberal Education," *Journal of General Education* 6:35-45, October 1951; "The Crisis in Contemporary Education," *Social Frontier* 5:140-45, February 1939; "Liberal Education—Theory and Practice," in *On General and Liberal Education: A Symposium*, pp. 14-18 (Washington: Association for General and Liberal Education, 1945); and the pages devoted to discussion of aspects of vocational education in Mortimer J. Adler and Milton S. Mayer, *The Revolution in Education* (Chicago: The University of Chicago Press, 1958). One who has time to examine only a few of the writings of Robert M. Hutchins would find it instructive to contrast his *The Higher Learning in America* (New Haven: Yale University Press, 1936) with a later book, *The Great Conversation: The Substance of a Liberal Education*, in *Great Books of the Western World* (54 vols. Chicago: Encyclopaedia Britannica, 1952). An instance of Hutchins' more recent statements of his perennial themes is *The University of Utopia* (Chicago: The University of Chicago Press, 1953) while two essays directly on the question of work and education are "The Place of Theological Education in a University," *Christian Education* 27:98-101, December 1943 and " 'Liberal' vs. 'Practical' Education—the Debate-of-the-Month," reprinted from *The Rotarian*, Vol. 69, 1946, in

C. Winfield Scott and Clyde M. Hill, editors, *Public Education under Criticism*, pp. 55-58 (New York: Prentice-Hall, 1954).

The principles that might guide those who wish to outline a Christian humanism of work have been suggested by, among others, Rudolf Allers, *Character Education in Adolescence*, pp. 157-65 (New York: Joseph F. Wagner, 1940); F. Charmot, *L'humanisme et l'humain*, pp. 69-79, 177-86, 285-98 (Paris: Editions Spes, 1934); and Jacques Maritain in his book, *Education at the Crossroads*, pp. 38, 45-46, 55-56 (New Haven: Yale University Press, 1943), as well as in his essay, "On Some Typical Aspects of Christian Education," in Edmund Fuller, editor, *The Christian Idea of Education*, pp. 187-98 (New Haven: Yale University Press, 1957). Georges Friedmann, *Pour l'unité de l'enseignement: Humanisme du travail et humanités* (Paris: Librairie Armand Colin, 1950) is a discussion bearing upon some of the concrete educational problems in this area. Practical pedagogical counsel for parents and teachers is offered by a number of brochures among which the following are typical: Jerome Count, *When Your Child Dislikes Work* (Pittsfield: Work Education Foundation, 1955); Edith G. Neisser, *Your Child's Sense of Responsibility* (Public Affairs Pamphlet No. 254. New York: Public Affairs Committee, 1957); and Ernest Osborne, *How To Teach Your Child about Work* (Public Affairs Pamphlet No. 216. New York: Public Affairs Committee, 1955). A great deal has been written about "work-experience" programs in the high school and much of this is summarized by DeWitt Hunt in *Work Experience Education Programs in American Secondary Schools* (Bulletin 1957, No. 5. Washington: U. S. Department of Health, Education, and Welfare). The appendix to this booklet provides a copious bibliography. An earlier publication on the same subject was Warren C. Seyfert and Paul A. Rehmus, editors, *Work Experience in Education* (Harvard Workshop Series: No. 2. Cambridge: Graduate School of Education, Harvard University, 1941). *The American Child*, Vol. 39, March 1957, an issue of the bi-monthly publication of the National Child Labor Committee in New York City, was devoted to "Work and Adolescent Development" and contained many brief, specific articles.

INDEX

Action, contemplation and, 7, 17, 153, 160, 176-79, 211
Adler, Felix, 156
Adler, Mortimer
  as student of John Erskine, 122
  at University of Chicago, 126-27
  biography and thought of, 95-100, 122-34
  educational theory of, 184
  Great Books of the Western World, 123, 129
  labor and leisure in theory of, 97, 129-31
  on aims of education, 117, 120
  on college program, 127
  on leisure, 98
  on manual work, 156
  on personality, 128
  rationalism of, 99, 128
  See also Hutchins, Robert Maynard
Adult education
  aims of, 210
  Great Books and, 133-34
  Hutchins and Adler on, 121-23, 129-30
  program of crafts in, 210
  traditional humanists and, 100
Agriculture, 138, 156
Allers, Rudolf
  Character Education in Adolescence, 156 *note*
  on humanistic values of work, 156, 158 *note*
  Psychology of Character, 158 *note*
Altruism, 111, 158
America
  attitudes toward work in, 18, 98, 146-47, 183, 194

conditions of work in, 67, 194
education in, 95-96, 117-20, 126, 127
possibilities for humanism of work in, 199
types of work in, 149
See also American civilization
American civilization
  effects of technology on, 75-77
  esteem of work in contemporary, 7, 18-19
  naturalism in, 33, 78
Ancient world, 181-82
Anthropology, Marxian speculations on, 27-28
Anti-Dühring, 35, 37
Aristotle
  attitude of toward manual labor, 5, 7
  Babbitt and, 114, 117
  influence of on modern education, 97
  on character education, 209
  on history, 107
  on intellectual operation, 80-81
  on speculative intelligence, 211
  Politics, 156
Art, 85, 90-91, 154-55
Asians, 10-11, 19-20
Atom Bomb and Education, 99 *note*
Autobiography of an Uneducated Man, 122
Avocation. *See* Occupational choice

Babbitt, Irving
  agreement of with Christianity, 138
  agreement of with Dewey, 105
  Aristotle and, 114, 117
  attitude of toward religion, 101, 103, 104, 105, 106, 114, 122